SOUTHERN TIMES

Contents

Front Cover: Reading - Redhill duty for N No 31867 on a sylvan summer's day. ***Ken Wightman / Transport Treasury***

Above: Our not really intended mystery picture provoked much comment, see page 78. By chance then, having established there are some who do still like a challenge, here is another location to identify. This time we do know where it is so no prize for a correct answer, just confirm your own knowledge...... .

Rear cover: Hastings unit No 1032 passing Three Oaks and Guestling Halt between Ore and Winchelsea. ***Gerald Daniels***

Copies of many of the images within SOUTHERN TIMES are available for purchase / download.

In addition the Transport Treasury Archive contains tens of thousands of other UK, Irish and some European railway photographs.

ISBN 978-1-913251-35-2

First Published in 2023 by Transport Treasury Publishing Ltd.,
16 Highworth Close, High Wycombe, HP13 7PJ

www.ttpublishing.co.uk *or for editorial issues and contributions email to* **southerntimes@email.com**

Printed in Tarxien, Malta by the Gutenberg Press Ltd.

INTRODUCTION

Welcome to Southern Times No 4. To those perhaps joining us for the first time – welcome (but where have you been...?) – if you have been with us 'from the past few stations' (for stations of course read 'issues'), I do hope you are enjoying the content.

Our aim is simple; to record history, some perhaps previously unreported, but also to present history in a new form, a form which we hope will not only appeal but also interest those who may not have known of the topic / subject previously. If in turn this stimulates further interest and individual research so much the better. None of us are here forever, I doubt for example there is anyone left who can recall the railways pre-1923 with any particular clarity and as if to emphasise that point we are fast running out of those who recall the Southern Railway before nationalisation – if you know someone who does remember that era please make the effort to speak to them, to report their stories and to preserve their memories. Don't let the past be consigned to the waste bin when they are gone and that includes physical paperwork and photographs. If we fail to do this all that will be left will be the bold facts and figures – useful of course – but hardly the full story.

Which brings me to my second point, the railway today. Standing on my local station ready to get the train to – it matters not – I was struck by how little of the past remains. In total honesty, apart from the route it takes, this is a totally different railway. Indeed, commencing with the ballast up, all has changed; the ballast shoulder is higher, there are concrete instead of wooden sleepers, flat bottom in lieu of bull-head track, breeze block supported platforms now with a tactile surface, a 'bus-shelter' waiting room, a disabled access footbridge (not that that is wrong), LED signals, no booking office, no platform staff, no goods yard, no signal box, and so on. All this on a site where 150 years ago was a brick built station, a station master, a busy goods yard, staff, etc, etc. And that is before we even come on to the train that arrived soon after.

Should I criticise – no. I am doing as I expect many of you also do which is to look at a similar scene through rose-tinted spectacles. All the more reason to attempt to hold on to and indeed confirm our memories by immersing ourselves in the articles and photographs in 'Southern Times' and similar publications.

For those who work on the railway today they can hardly imagine what it would have been like 50-60 years ago, for that is when times did start to change, the previous century before seeing little major adjustment compared with the revolution of the late 20th and 21st. What I find amazing, and I write this as someone who has reached his 'three-score years and ten', is how to the younger enthusiast railways still hold a fascination, but I am genuinely pleased they do. (Do I dare admit to having a slight admiration for the sheer pulling power of a Class 66?) Perhaps in a few decades' time they too will look back on something like fixed LED signals with nostalgia - assuming that is fixed signals will have disappeared in lieu of in-cab signalling – and perhaps consider fondly that what to them was once called a 'train station' but has now been renamed a 'railway station'; after all, does all life not go round in circles...?

Kevin Robertson and the team at The Transport Treasury.

The next issue of SOUTHERN TIMES, No 5, will be available in May 2023

Contents to include: The original LBSCR Motor-Trains, John Davenport Part 2, Staines to Wokingham (and beyond), Southern Region people, Holland Park Halt, the Adams 135 - 146 class, Stephen Townroe in colour, and of course lots more.

MAIN LINE.

PRIVATE.—For the use of the Company's Servants only.

LONDON & SOUTH WESTERN RAILWAY.

WORKING TIME TABLES

OF

PASSENGER AND GOODS TRAINS

For APRIL, 1884.

Each person supplied with a Copy of these Tables is held responsible that he reads carefully, and obeys, all Notices and Instructions contained therein so far as they concern him. No excuse of want of knowledge can be admitted for any Failure or Neglect of Duty.

Errors or inaccuracies must be pointed out to the Traffic Superintendent without delay.

Where the times of arrival and departure are not both shown in these Tables, the time shown is the departure time.

NOTICE.—The figures (between waved lines) thus 10 50 or (with a line between) thus

arr.	dep.
10	50

show the time at which Trains that do not stop should pass the Stations or Junctions.

The places marked —— show where Trains are to pass one another. The places marked ▬ show that the Train does not proceed further on the same Line.

FOR ALTERATIONS OF TRAINS FOR APRIL, 1884, SEE PAGES 3 & 4.

For Trains on the Waterloo and Kingston, Shepperton, Hammersmith and New Richmond, Windsor and Reading, Ludgate Hill and Richmond, Nine Elms, Willesden and Brent, and Waterloo and Willesden North Western Train Service, see separate Service Book headed Windsor Line.

LONDON:
WATERLOW & SONS LIMITED, PRINTERS, LONDON WALL.

S. W. Main 1

The Good Old Days

We were recently given the privilege of taking on custody of a few items of paperwork and photographs from the collection of a deceased enthusiast. It was not a large archive, but, no matter what, it was indeed appreciated and included a copy of the LSWR 'Main Line Working Timetable ' covering passenger and goods services for April 1884. Indeed, it was this very item that gave the idea for the theme of the introduction to this issue – hence also for follow on as the first article. For those of a particular age, the term 'The Good Old Days' was also the name of a BBC television series which ran from 1953 until 1983, the acts and audience dressing in period costume.

But are we again looking at things with our proverbial rose-tinted viewpoint? I would venture to say yes. Going back several years the late Barry Curl had a book published, 'The LSWR at Nine Elms' (Kestrel Railway Books 2004). Included in this were examples from Charles Booth's poverty maps, coloured maps of London describing the living conditions and social structure of various areas of London, including in the case in question, examples of the area around Nine Elms.

The Booth maps were coded according to the status / standing of the streets and residents and which for interest today were:

Yellow – Upper middle class and middle class. Wealthy.

Red – Middle class. Well to do.

Pink – Fairly comfortable. Good ordinary earnings.

Purple – Mixed. Some comfortable, others poor.

Light Blue - Poor. 18s. to 21s. a week for a moderate family.

Dark Blue - Very poor, casual. Chronic want.

Black - Lowest class. Vicious, semi-criminal.

As to where a railwayman fitted into this social scale is open to debate, pink, purple or light blue would seem to be the most likely but this could change so easily due to any number of factors. The area in which they lived, the number in the family the wage earner was responsible for, and most of all his earnings.

In the case of footplate staff, earnings were dictated principally by seniority, a newly promoted driver clearly earning less than a senior man. But so much could also depend on the actions of that same man during his daily work and, consequently, it is here that we now turn again to the 1884 timetable for within, and clearly included as a warning to employees under the heading 'Lists of Punishments', was the following detail:

An Engine Driver and Fireman have been fined for losing time with their Train.

An Engine Driver has been fined for disregarding signals. Crossing Gates broken in consequence.

An Engine Driver has been fined for omitting to stop at a Station when booked to do so.

An Engine Driver has been fined for running past Signals when at danger, thereby causing a collision.

An Engine Driver and Fireman have been fined for allowing the lead plug of Engine to melt out.

An Engine Driver has been fined for making out Train Ticket incorrectly.

Several Engine Drivers have been fined for-running a station platform.

An Inspector and Pointsman have been fined for throwing a tender off the rails.

A Guard has been fined for throwing wagons off the road.

A Guard has been fined for wrongly booking time of train.

An Assistant Guard has been fined for leaving a passenger behind.

A Signalman has been fined for throwing vehicles off the road.

A Shunter has been fined for throwing a carriage off the rails.

A Head Porter has been fined for causing damage to a carriage.

Several porters have been fined for coming late to duty.

A Porter has been fined for travelling without a pass or ticket.

A Porter has been fined for causing crossing gates to be broken.

A Porter has been fined for damaging a tail lamp in shunting.

A Porter has been fined for carelessness and neglect of duty.

A Porter has been dismissed for misconduct towards a passenger, and travelling without a pass or ticket.

A Ballast Train Foreman has been fined for careless working of a Ballast Train, thereby causing damage to a crane.

A Ballast Train Flagman has been fined for careless working of a Ballast Train, thereby causing damage to a crane.

A Ganger has been fined for careless working of a trolley.

A Ganger and Platelayer have been fined for improperly attaching a trolley to a train.

Without the full circumstances it would be unwise to draw specific conclusions whilst the locations, dates and any extenuating circumstances are similarly not reported. Penalties appear mainly to have been in monetary terms except of course for those wretched individuals dismissed as a result. Of all, one that on the surface does appear particularly harsh was the fine issued to a porter for damaging a hand lamp – surely there must be more to this one.

Whilst discipline and compliance with the rules was essential to railway staff, in the case of a derailment or incident there was little worker representation available to the staff, employment was thus tenuous and by losing his job consequently a man might go down the social scale extremely quickly.

Opposite: Damage to a tender; no details or date given. The particular individual to whom blame might be apportioned for such an event could expect little mercy at this time in history. The consequences of demotion or even sacking in which case social circumstances of the individual and their family as references by 'Booth' might well change, literally overnight.
Curl Collection

Above: Damage to a Radial tank, possibly No 106. Both this and the previous view were taken at Nine Elms pending repair.
Curl Collection

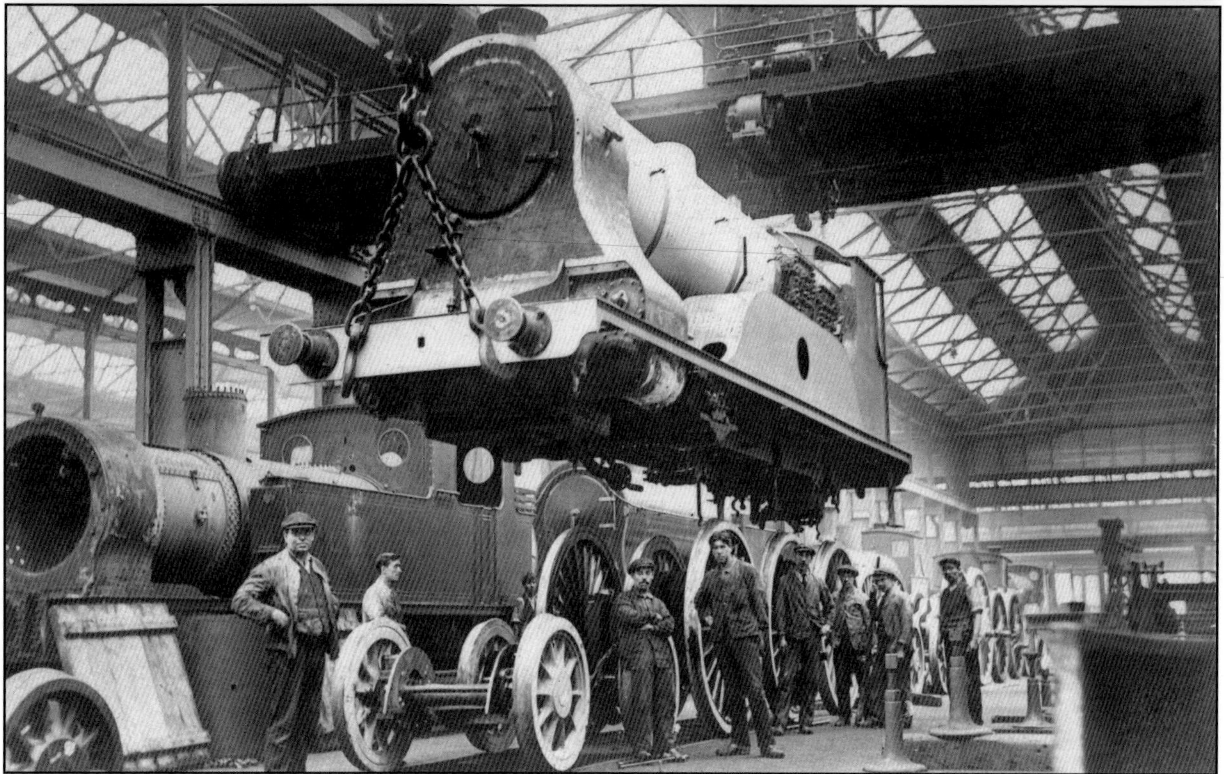

The LSWR T14 class (The Paddlebox')

The 4-6-0 wheel arrangement took a little time to become established in the UK as a prime mover although by the early years of the 20th century, with increasing loads and a need to increase speed, there were a number of companies producing steam designs of this type. We have to be fair and say probably the most successful of these was the GWR with their 'Saint' and, soon after, 'Star' classes, both setting the standard for GWR locomotive policy until the end of steam of what was then the WR.

The very first 4-6-0 steam engine was reported in America as early in 1849 whilst in the UK it was the Highland Railway with their 'Jones Goods' of 1894 that led the way. This was followed by the North Eastern (1899), Great Central (1902), Great Western (1902), London & North Western (1903), and Great Eastern (1912) railways.

Dugald Drummond of the LSWR had entered the field with a 4-6-0 design, the 'F13' class in 1905. This was followed by the 'E14' in 1907, and then the 'G14' and 'P14' types in 1908. Although most were reasonably successful the proportionate increase in size from his highly successful 4-4-0 types did not necessarily equal a proportionate increase in performance and despite in some cases rebuilding by Drummond's successor, Robert Urie, all had ceased work by the end of 1927 – the solitary 'E14' 4-6-0 having a life of only just over six years.

The one exception to this sad story was the 'T14' design, another 4-6-0 dating from 1911, ten being built, nine of which survived into British Railways days – just – the tenth example consigned to scrap following an enemy air raid on Nine Elms in 1940.

Numerically, the ten locomotives of the T14 type took the numbers 443 to 447 and 458 to 462, the gap in the middle occupied by F14 class Nos 448 to 452 and G14 Nos 453 to 457.

Aesthetically the T14 design bore a distinct family familiarity to the preceding 4-6-0 by Drummond although it must also be stressed mechanically and performance wise there were considerable variations in the LSWR 4-6-0 designs.

Drummond had likely believed that by adding an extra pair of coupled wheels and thereby increasing the length of the boiler, plus the addition of cross firebox tubes to further add to the heating surface, a well performing engine would result. Sadly he was to be mistaken as the firebox was now insufficient to feed the boiler, the cross tubes taking up too much space for little if any advantage whilst in addition the ashpan did not permit admission of sufficient air. The front end steam passages were also far from ideal.

In consequence the water and particularly the coal consumption was excessive, on occasions double what might have been expected, whilst it took a highly skilled and competent fireman to deal with the firebox.

Various modifications were made both under Drummond and later under his successor Urie, but the class never rose to the standards that had been expected and the fastest trains reverted to 4-4-0 haulage, a situation that would continue until the advent of the King Arthur class. The 4-6-0s meanwhile found

Opposite top: A member of the T14 class under construction at Eastleigh in 1911 / 12. The actual engine is not identified but realistically it is most likely one of the early builds, perhaps even the doyen, No 443, in which case this would likely be the early months of 1911. It would usually be practice to record the first of a new type. Above the running plate the engine appears basically complete and will probably soon be ready to be hoisted into the air, ready for the wheels to be added. The position of the valve chests may be seen. This is also one of the few views available that depict the right-hand side of the loco. *Curl Collection*

Opposite bottom: Hoisted high in the air and stationary to allow the necessary exposure of the period. Driving wheel and bogie are ready to be added whilst it may be noted the smokebox door and buffers have now been added. A variety of other Adams and Drummond locomotives are receiving attention in the background. *Commercial postcard*

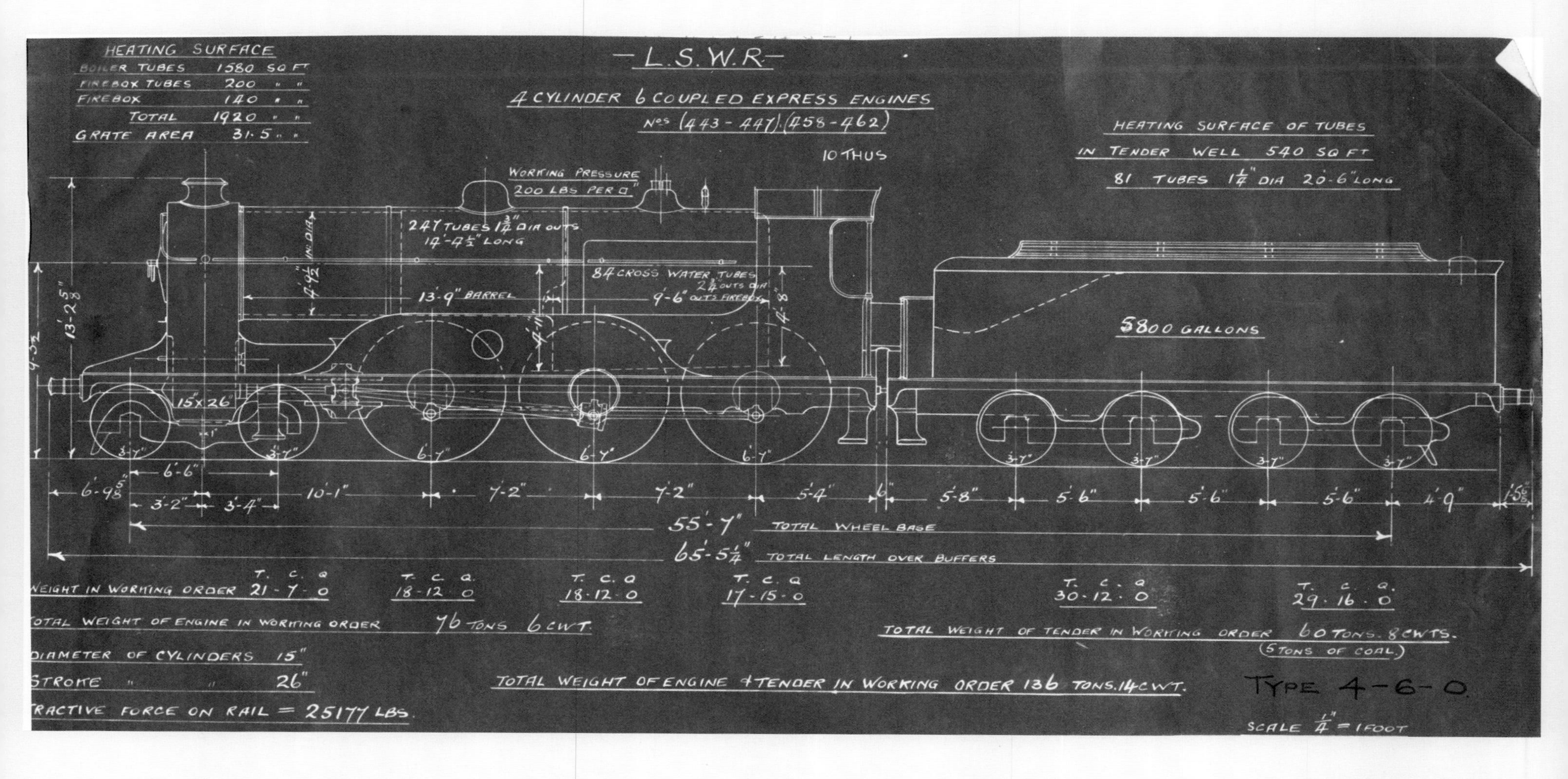

There is an interesting reference on the drawing. top-right, to ' Heating surface of tubes in tender well 540 sq ft. 81 tubes 1¼" dia. and 20' 6" long.' This is not explained further. Note also, the original blueprint is cut-off slightly on the left hand edge.

work on lesser duties as well as heavy freight for which they were found eminently suitable.

Last, and certainly the most successful of the Drummond 4-6-0 types, were the ten engines of the T14 class. Again there was a marked similarity to what had gone before with firebox cross tubes whilst a similar boiler, but pitched higher, was carried. The four cylinders were also now in line horizontally, resulting in a massive saddle which also supported the smokebox. The sides of the smokebox also followed a gentle outward curve to the running plate encasing the outside of the piston vales. Viewed from the front they quickly gained the nickname 'double breasters' although at some time the latter appears to have fallen out of use to be replaced by 'paddlebox'. With the top of the running plate extending back on the same level from the buffer beam, aesthetically they presented a massive appearance enhanced by the higher pitched boiler and the top third of the driving wheels covered.

Performance was reasonable although again skilled firing was required for if an amount of coal were to develop towards the front of the grate, steam pressure, and with it performance, would quickly falter. Under these circumstances recourse might have to be made to an 11 feet fire iron, no mean feat on a moving engine. By inference Bradley implies this was really only satisfactorily dealt with when the then engine came to its next booked stop – and by now of course behind time.

Away again it might be anticipated that the driver would attempt to make up time but the class suffered from inadequate bearing surfaces and hot boxes were a frequent difficulty.

Under Urie, and with a real need for a capable 4-6-0, modifications were made to No 458

Class	Cylinder size	Driving wheels	Performance	History
F13 (5 engines)	16 x 24 (4)	6' 0"	Poor steaming	Scrapped
E14 (1 engine)	16½ x 24 (4)	6' 0"	V poor steaming	Rebuilt as H15 4-6-0
G14 (5 engines)	15 x 24 (4)	6' 0"	Some improvement but rarely exceeded best 4-4-0 designs.	Officially engines rebuilt into 'King Arthur' class but probably little excepting the tenders was used.
P14 (5 engines)	15 x 24 (4)	6' 0" Wheelbase and inside piston valves difference to P14 type		
T14	15 x 24 (4)	6' 7"	Higher boiler pressure (200 psi) (previous 4-6-0 types had been 175 psi) and a steam dryer improved the performance but they required skilled firing.	

443
L S W R

which included the removal of the Drummond steam dryer and its replacement with a superheater for which the smokebox was also extended ahead of the front of the saddle. The firebox cross tubes were also removed. Results obtained justified the cost of the changes and the remaining nine were similarly dealt with.

The type continued working semi-fast and relief duties, including Waterloo – Southampton services via Alton; it would be interesting to know how they performed on the 1-60 gradients on this line. Hot boxes however still plagued the design but this was effectively cured under Maunsell by the simple expedient of raising the running plate so as to expose the axle boxes to a greater draught when travelling; the visual change that resulted reducing their top heavy appearance. More important than mere aesthetics was the fitting of Maunsell type superheaters and mechanical lubricators. All had been so dealt with by May 1933.

Probably the highlight of their work on regular services was when one of the class was booked for the Up Bournemouth Belle in the summer of 1934/35. The Down train had its usual 'King Arthur' in charge but the Up was poorly patronised and consequently given over to a 'Paddlebox'

Opposite: Accompanying the blueprint shown on the previous spread was this view of the completed No 443 – left hand side again – recorded at Eastleigh. All four cylinders were in line but meaning the valves, as seen here on the left-hand side, had to be driven from above the running plate. Workshop grey livery, with the circular window in the splasher a common feature on the Drummond 4-6-0 types. Its purpose was to allow access for lubrication.

Right: Cab view. Basic controls and steam reverse. The firehole door has flaps slightly reminiscent of a baker's oven; firing likely a knack so as to avoid the raised areas, the largest of which is an internal splasher for the rear driving wheels. ***Curl Collection***

whilst the King Arthur took an ordinary but heavier working.

With the cascading of Schools class engines away from the Portsmouth line following electrification in the summer of 1937, their days might well have been expected to be numbered although Eastleigh had major spares in the form of two spare fireboxes and a set of cylinders to hand. Nos 458 and 461 were the fortunate recipients in late 1937. Bulleid, in his role of the new CME, instructed that no further spares were to be provided and consequently No 443 was the first to be condemned due to defective cylinders on 5 January 1938. The deteriorating political situation saw the order rescinded and new cylinders were fitted with the engine returning to traffic in March 1938. It would last for a further 11 years.

By that time, duties included milk trains and stopping passenger turns. Upon the outbreak of war unknown class members also worked evacuation trains from London and Southampton west to Brockenhurst, Christchurch, Bournemouth and Poole. Three, Nos 444,446 and 460, were initially placed in store around this time, with two others, Nos 459 and 461, engaged on carriage heating at Clapham Junction. All were subsequently reinstated for general service. As might also be expected their duties also increased as war progressed, taking over both passenger and freight workings, including petrol tanker specials, the freight workings involving work to Reading, Willesden and Neasden. Four engines of the class were based at Feltham in 1943/4. Again according to Bradley, No 462 was noted as far west as Exmouth Junction shed on 17 November 1944.

No 445 at speed possibly near Earlsfield – right-hand side view! Dependent upon the period, pre- or post-1921, this is either a Waterloo – Guildford, or Waterloo – Southampton service. (The white area close to the track below the buffer is not escaping steam but a blemish on the original print.)

Top: No 458 as modified by Urie with an extended smokebox to accommodate superheating. Other changes include the removal of the firebox cross tubes, external clack boxes and a Urie style smokebox door. Photographed at Nine Elms.

Right: Additional alteration by Maunsell with the covering below the running plate removed so allowing greater access to the outside valve gear and the superheater replaced by one of Maunsell type. Snifting valves added. The 'E' prefix carried by this engine was removed in November 1931, all of the class with this letter similarly altered between 1931 and 1933.

Opposite: Salisbury, Basingstoke or Bournemouth are the most likely destinations for this unidentified member of the class setting off from Waterloo in August 1948 with a Bulleid brake as the first vehicle of the train. ***T. Rendell / Transport Treasury***

Above: Routine servicing at Eastleigh – the rear of the houses of Campbell Road on the right. Left is Adams '0395' No 566 and on the right T14 No 444, the latter having its tender replenished. ***HNS / Transport Treasury***

Under Maunsell's tenure, the external livery had been lined green, but from mid-1940 onwards repaints were in unlined green, and subsequently black, the latter commencing with No 446 in August 1941. The last to go into black was No 459 in June 1945.

Another external change was the fitting of a Urie type stovepipe – similar to those carried by the Urie G16 and H16 tank classes – to No 447 in October 1940; Eastleigh unable to supply the regular replacement. No 458 had been the only one to retain its original fitting but not for long as it was seriously damaged (along with Lord Nelson No 852) by enemy action at Nine Elms on 30 September / 1 October 1940. No 852 was repaired – more like almost a new engine – but No 447 was not so lucky and condemned, likely yielding some parts for the remaining engines.

The remaining nine survived WW2, indeed six were to receive heavy overhauls in 1945/46, including fireboxes and cylinders. The latter especially were probably long overdue for overhaul, again quoting Bradley, '.... By this date (1944) all were filthy dirty and often in such poor mechanical condition that the front end was continually shrouded in steam and the exhaust beat so irregular that instead of four beats per revolution there was a roar, two feeble grunts and a gasp. Even so they appear to have been able to be relied upon for despite losing time on Saturday relief services post-war they did at least reach their intended destinations; which was often more than the modern Bulleid types managed around the same time.'

By this time their days were definitely numbered although three received BR

30119
447

identification as Nos 30446, 30461 and 30447; the first two being repainted in plain black with 'British Railways' on the tender.

Three of the nine went in 1948, two in 1949, two in 1950 and the final two in 1951.

Opposite top: The end for No 458 in the carnage that was Nine Elms the morning after the raid of 30 September / 1 October 1940 that resulted in the engine being condemned. Whilst at first glance the damage may not appear to be too severe, the engine had in fact taken much of the force of a 250lb high-explosive bomb and so extensive was the damage that a breaking-up order was issued just three days later. 'Lord Nelson' No 852 was standing on an adjacent road within the shed and although extensively damaged in the same incident was repaired – see article in Issue 2 of *Southern Times.*

Opposite bottom: Early BR days at Nine Elms. No 447 stands company with No 30119 and what may possibly be a 'King Arthur'. This was one of just three of the class that were to be renumbered with '30' added to their SR identification. It would remain in service until December 1949. To the writer, the visual appeal of the class has to be in the old-fashioned appearance created by the curved 'wings' at the front. The protruding smokebox enhancing the overall effect. Because their demise was early, none survived the dismantling process.

Above: Still at work on a Salisbury service at Vauxhall on 8 July 1949. No 444 (not renumbered by British Railways) in charge of the 12.54pm Down working. Bradley described the working of the class post-war in general terms as, 'Despite the presence of Merchant Navy and West Country Pacifics, Nos 443/6/7/60-62 appeared regularly on the summer Saturday reliefs in 1946-7 and, although often losing time, nevertheless reached their destinations, which was more than many of their modern replacements achieved.' Certainly No 444 appears to be performing reasonably well with a feather of steam at the safety valve although how long this will be retained west of Clapham is not certain. Much depended of course on the type of coal, the boiler / firebox and the willingness of the fireman. The late John Click recounts an incident in which he describes the sound made by the T14 class. Referring to his runs involving the trials of No 36001 he comments, 'For the dynamometer car tests at Eastleigh I rode on No 36001, in the fireman's cab usually, and kept darting into the bunker to tip weighed bags of coal out on to the shovelling plate as required. Near Fleet one night there was a sudden crescendo of new sound. I made my way along the corridor to report, only to find that we had just overtaken a T14 'Paddlebox' 4-6-0 which had attempted to have a race with us on the slow line. What a sight that would have been in the half-light! With only half a central cab (on 'Leader') we were blind to the 'double-breaster!"

Loco number	Date Built (Eastleigh	Fitted with large tender	Superheated	Maunsell modifications	Withdrawn and disposal	Mileage
(30) 443	5/1911	7/1912	11/1915	7/1931	5/1949 Scrapped Elh.	1,014,996
(30) 444	5/1911	7/1912	7/1917	3/1931	2/1950 Scrapped Elh.	
(30) 445	6/1911	8/1912	12/1915	2/1931	10/1949 Scrapped Dinton	
(30) 446	6/1911	9/1912	11/1915	8/1931	4/1951 Scrapped Elh.	
(30) 447	7/1911	10/1912	2/1917	9/1930	12/19 Scrapped Elh.49	1,103,419
458	12/1911	12/1912	8/1915	11/1930	10/1940 Scrapped Nine Elms	846,752
(30) 459	7/1912	7/1912	5/1917	12/1930	11/1948 Scrapped Dinton	1,044,200
(30) 460	2/1912	12/1/1912	9/1916	4/1930	11/1948 Scrapped Dinton	
(30) 461	4/1912	1/1913	2/1918	6/1931	8/1951 Scrapped Elh.	1,054,621
(30) 462	5/1912	5/1912	10/1917	8/1930	2/1950 Scrapped Elh.	

As BR No 30461 at Woking on an Up freight: 9.10am, 14 July 1949. It is not believed the type ever ventured away from the Western section of the Southern. ***Transport Treasury***

Book Review:
'Many and Great Inconveniences.....'

There are four societies that I am aware of specifically supporting the memory of the constituents and the Southern Railway, respectively, The South Western Circle, The Brighton Circle, The South Eastern & Chatham Railway Society, and the Southern Railways Group (if we have left anybody out, sincere apologies). In addition there are support groups for the various heritage lines operating in the Southern area and preserved Southern area locomotives.

Of those named, the South Western Circle has probably been the most prolific so far as publication is concerned and by this we do not refer to the members' magazines that appear from each on a regular basis.

The latest of these from the SWC is 'Many and Great Inconveniences. The Level Crossings and Gatekeepers' Cottages of the Southampton & Dorchester Railway' compiled by Philip A. Brown. Exactly how Philip has managed to secure so much information on what to many might appear to be an obscure subject – and to be totally honest it is – but no matter, what he has produced is a comprehensive and fascinating account of the need for, the detail of, and the history of the 40 or so places where a road or track crossed the Southampton & Dorchester Railway on its curved route via Ringwood and Wimborne and where a level crossing was provided. Indeed, to the best of my knowledge this is the first time such an in- depth study of such a feature has been undertaken for any railway company.

Without wishing to sound like a repetitive television advert, the SWC have produced a number of what they refer to as 'monographs' on various subjects ranging from the Salisbury Accident of 1906, to Feltham Yard, Beattie locomotives, Waterloo Signalling to name but a few, plus now this new work; a much enlarged edition of an earlier monograph. Members receive each new monograph free - to be fair the publication and members'

offered to a mainstream publisher, would no doubt have received scant attention.

Publication of such works is exactly the role of societies like the SWC and both they and Philip Brown are to be commended.

'The Level Crossings and Gatekeepers' Cottages of the Southampton & Dorchester Railway' is written by Philip A. Brown and published by The South Western Circle. 212 pages, A5 size, printed on art paper with both colour and b/w illustrations. Details from the society at www.lswr.org

36001

Track Spreading by 'Leader'

In my last and final book on what will probably always be my pet subject, I categorically stated, '...this was it...no more...'. At the time a genuine statement but then I had not taken into account an email and subsequent correspondence with long time railway friend Bill Allen and through whom I was privileged to speak to Francis Terry and who in turn referred me to someone he knew, John Savage.

Bill and Terry had met in consequence on holiday and discussion quickly established both had a lasting railway interest. It was in consequence of this conversation that I was fortunate to correspond with Francis and be passed a brief file of papers, the covers of which were already showing signs of deterioration. The notation on the edge reads, 'Flange Force Measuring Leader loco.'

Now at this stage we should bring in a previously published history and where on p148 of the 1977 Ian Allan book 'Bulleid of the Southern', written by Bulleid's son, H A V (Antony) Bulleid, he states when referring to Leader on trial from Brighton, 'There were also murmurings that the engine had spread the track, but these were never substantiated.' Up to now that has been the only place where any such allegation has been made and we must make to comment that allegations - in any walk of life – are easy to make but not only sometimes hard to substantiate but equally sometimes hard to refute. (Similar allegations had been made years earlier against the Gresley P2 2-8-2 locos at work in Scotland.) Similarly an allegation/slur/accusation without foundation can also cause sometimes irreparable damage to the reputation of an inanimate object - a piece of machinery - and of course an individual.

So might there now be some truth in the allegations of track spreading by Leader and if so what and who from? To answer such questions let me first say that I have been reluctant to repeat them in print previously for the simple reason of the lack of any corroborating evidence. And as to who might have been responsible, we have to say this can only have come from the office of the Chief Civil Engineer of the Southern Region in charge of the lines out of Brighton and in particular that running east towards Lewes. He in turn would have received such information from his Permanent Way Inspectors and further down the food chain, the actual ganger responsible for a piece of line.

In order to cover all angles and be as objective as possible, for these are indeed serious allegations, we first of all need to look at the engine itself and where we know there was a definite imbalance between the weights on the axleboxes on either side – due primarily to the offset boiler allowing more weight on one side than the other. In addition, lack of sufficient movement in the horns could similarly have accentuated the problem. In short we have all the ingredients for extra pressure being applied to one side of the rails and we should also remember the balance weights – several tons of pig iron – had yet to be added to the corridor side (this was only done before the trials at Eastleigh), also that the line between Brighton and Lewes is subject to several reverse curves which Leader might well be taking other than at shall we say 'walking pace'.

A Times image of No 36001 from late 1949 with the engine descending the reverse curves of Falmer bank. (The press photographer would most likely have made with British Railways to ascertain when the engine was – hopefully - running and on which lines.) No other newspapers appear to have shown any images of the engine around this period. Folklore has it that when signalman were alerted, in consequence of a special traffic weekly or daily notice that the engine was running, they would advise nearby residents in advance to take in any washing; Leader being known to throw sparks and cinders over a wide area. At this time in history the lateral forces being exerted on the curves were likely not even being considered. They would only come to light as a result of the regular on the ground inspections by the local ganger.
Colourisation by David Williams

So to the actual file. The first few pages are simply contemporary photostat copies from the 6 January 1950 issue of 'The Engineer' comprising a brief description of 'the Leader' engine. This is followed by two pages of hand written mathematical calculations - as was then practice these are written on the reverse of earlier unrelated memorandums (the railway would maximise the use of materials) and, after this, two double page reports and a single page memorandum.

The first is dated 10 January 1950 and is addressed to the Assistant Civil Engineer from an unknown individual on the Southern Region and at an unknown office - almost certainly London somehow. The importance of the comments made are also such that much needs to be reported verbatim:

'Referring to the Mechanical and Electrical Engineer's letter of 3 January to the Chief Civil Engineer, I have been in touch with Mr Nettell of the Electrical Engineer's Office, London Bridge, in an endeavour to fix this meeting which was originally to be held today.

'When I first met Mr Burrows' clerk, I informed him that Mr Wells of the Electrical Engineer's staff accompanied Mr Dean and myself to Paris in 1946 for the purpose of studying work done by the SNCF on the oscillation of electric locomotives and the recording of their side thrusts, and that it seemed to me that Mr Wells and any others concerned might usefully be drawn into this meeting since I understand that they had been pursuing the design and acquisition of apparatus for this purpose. This suggestion was readily accepted but has complicated the matter of fixing a mutually convenient meeting date. The meeting will not be held this week and I am awaiting a revised date.

'I telephoned Mr Parker's office to ascertain from him more details of the damage done to the track between Lewes and Brighton and I give details below, data supplied by Mr Mansbridge of his office.

1 - The track between Brighton and Lewes is nearly all curved with short straight lengths in between, and gauge spreading has occurred on both straight and curved track.

2 - Cause may be due to either loco oscillation or bogie stiffness. It is not known which.

3 - Side cutting has been confined almost without exception to the high rail when on curved track.

4 - The ganger has stated the speed was well over 60mph although the speed limit between Brighton and Lewes is 55mph.

5 - No trouble has been experienced between Lewes and Groombridge probably owing to very much lower speeds on this line.

6 - They have no information other than that given in their letter to the Chief Civil Engineer dated 15 December 1949.

7 - Spread on the straight not so severe (1/8") but on both sides alternately. Curves are all high rail push out about 3/8" max.'

The report is initialled but the individual letters are not discernible.

One week later, on 17 January, is a second report, this time of a meeting held at Brighton on 17 January. Again the participants are not mentioned, but the information is, most telling.

'A Leader class engine, and the axle box arrangement in particular, was examined. Differences in the construction of Leader class locomotives and other locomotives was discussed. Particulars regarding tyre profiles, bogie suspension and control, spring deflection, etc, etc, were noted.

'It was decided:

1 - That the track, where widening of the gauge had occurred, should be examined as soon as possible, and arrangements were made for an examination to be carried out on 27 January, those concerned to meet at Brighton at 10.00am.

2 - That useful information might be obtained if a trial run were made with the engine on the same track, any effects on the track being especially noted.

This photograph first appeared in *The Times* on 4 November 1949 under the heading 'A new type of British Locomotive'. Aside from the build details the information given was almost all correct. It showed a test train running between Lewes and Seaford. "A new and unusual type of locomotive, the Leader class 0-6-6-0 six-cylinder tank engine driving two power bogies, undergoing tests near Lewes. Making a departure from British locomotive design, it has a driving cab at each end connected by a corridor, to obviate the turn-round. The fireman's cab is in the middle. Five of these locomotives are being completed at the Eastleigh works of British Railways." The article appears not to have provoked any comment at the time being merely a news story, but later in 1953 the same photograph would be used in the *Sunday Despatch* complete with exaggerated and inaccurate reporting. Sensationalism and factual distortion is not limited to late 20th and 21st century news and television media either, for the same view reproduced in another book states 'The fireman is having a breather' (referring to the heat within). Certainly at first glance it does appear as if someone is leaning from the centre cab; closer examination however reveals it is in fact an elbow, with the body of the individual facing inbound. The sliding centre door is partly open – No. 1 end is leading. *Colourisation by David Williams*

3 - That in the meantime one of Mr Smyth's assistants should visit Brighton to examine a Leader class locomotive and ascertain whether flange force could be measured by the application of strain gauge methods.'

There matters rested until the final report dated 26 January 1950, the start of which at least may be summarised more simply. We learn at least three individuals visited Brighton on 19 January to look into the possibility of measuring the lateral forces set up between the rail by Leader and also 'conventional' types of locomotive. The trio also visited the works at Eastleigh and similarly '...discussed the problem with the Research Section at Ashford.' 'In general it was thought that the conventional types of locomotive could be tackled fairly easily but that the Leader was a far more difficult proposition.'

The party went on to say regarding Leader, 'The difficulties in this type of locomotive (in measuring the lateral forces) are accentuated because of the very small side play and because of the rugged construction of the axle box and guides.'

The report also contained recommendations:

'It is suggested that experiments should be started forthwith along the lines described on one of the spare pairs of Leader wheels, axles and axle boxes now lying in the Eastleigh Loco works…..'

But as with all reports, without access to the other paperwork referred to in this one report, it is not easy to reach every conclusion but we certainly can with some.

Firstly, contrary to H.A.V. Bulleid's words, I think we can with reasonable certainty say Leader did spread the track, at least between Brighton and Lewes.

The comments about it being easier to check for movement with a conventional locomotive are also interesting; are we then to believe difficulties had occurred in the past with other types of engine, and if so, which ones, where and when? The papers give no indication on this course.

Comment is made about the robust construction of the bogies and limited side play on Leader, could this be anything to do with the use of chains for the final drive? What we are not told is if measurements were taken - and they surely would have been - relative to the wear profile of the tyres on Leader. In the opinion of the present writer, the offset drive of Leader might seem to imply it would be the centre axle alone which would have been the most likely to cause side cutting, being the one restricted by a drive chain on either side.

Next we come to the point that the party refer to when visiting Eastleigh works and examining. On the 19 January they talk about the commencement of tests on '…some of the spare pairs of Leader wheels, axles, and axle boxes now lying in the Eastleigh Loco Works'. In short how did they get there? (And equally why were they there?) The conclusion has to be they were new stock intended for use on No 36004/5 and had yet to be shipped to Brighton - recall all work on the remaining engines, Nos 36002-36005, had been curtailed by Riddles in November 1949 and as we know the wheelsets were constructed at Eastleigh; they must have been simply lying around awaiting a decision as to their future.

The whole issue of timescales also needs examining in detail. The engine was built at Brighton (erected might be more strictly accurate with some components made at both Eastleigh and Ashford). Up to this time, all its trials had been from Brighton and with two exceptions, when the route was to Eastleigh, every other trial had 'turned right' at Brighton and taken the route to Lewes - and wherever after that.

Between 13 December and 27 January it only ran on three occasions, once to Crowborough and Oxted (via the Brighton - Lewes line), once to Tealight and then again once more via Lewes to Tunbridge Wells.

Between 27 January and 13 April it was mostly stored save for one light engine trip to Eastleigh in early February. In March it never left Brighton.

So, conclusions. The limited physical movement of the engine during the December / January 1949/1950 period corresponds exactly to the time scale of the paperwork in the file. It is reasonable to conclude the Chief Civil Engineer had become aware of the allegations of track spreading (and for 'spreading' we might equally replace with 'damage'), and thus likely it was prohibited from further trials.

Bulleid was still notionally on the Southern Region at this time but it is interesting to note his name is not referred to nor indeed does he appear to have been consulted, confirmation he was being marginalised.

It also gives corroboration to the rumour it was the CCE of the Central Section who was not prepared to accept further trials of the engine, hence then the move to Eastleigh, but Riddles at BRB Headquarters must have been aware and yet even with what is almost certain proof of major difficulties he authorised further trials - but now from Eastleigh and with a definite 50mph speed limit.

I have mentioned before, Leader was effectively condemned even before it ever turned a wheel. The early BR era was not the time for an innovative design of the like of Leader, instead it was a time of consolidation and more gentle experimentation, particularly so with traction other than steam.

It is unlikely the issues with the riding of Leader and consequential track damage could have been resolved without a major redesign and starting of course with a more centralised weight perspective. Sadly yet another reason to condemn what a bold initiative but one which ritualistically never had a chance of survival.

(The file from which this article has been compiled were literally saved from the skip well in to the privatisation era.)

Caption - no similar issues seem to have been reported working from Eastleigh. The Turf Burner was not affected and here the weight was centralised.

(The original file will be preserved as an important record of contemporary railway history. It has been passed to the Bluebell Archive for safe keeping.)

Unconnected with the previous, but here might also be an appropriate time to mention a note recently received from Simon Baker concerning a certain publication on the Leader. Simon comments, 'On page 200 there is a view of the cab on No 36001. The wheel valve on the lower right is for the steam heating system, the valve is the same as on the Bulleid Pacifics. The steam heat safety valve is visible on its cast bronze 'tee' with the steam supply to the steam heat gauge between the two items.' Simon concludes with, 'I wonder if one of the two large pressure gauges shown are for the boiler instead of two steam chest gauges'. (The reason for my own comment about the engine having two steam chest pressure gauges was simply due to the presence of two separate steam chests – one on each bogie. Likely we may now never know.)

A Horsham to Guildford service entering Christ's Hospital behind M7 No 30051. The Guildford bound platform was equipped with two platform faces, a not uncommon feature at various locations on the system generally, but nowadays rare – although one was still extant at Guildford in 2022.

This time it is a train in the opposite direction. A Guildford to Horsham freight recorded at Rudgwick; C2X No 32541 in charge.

A Surrey-Sussex line: Horsham to Guildford Part 2

(Part 1 appeared in Issue No 3)

Upon his father's death, George, the Garman's eldest son, succeeded him as senior porter-signalman at Slinfold. Four of Mrs. Garman's six sons started their careers on the railway, and she believes they all started at Slinfold Station. It is a wonderful record and one that I imagine is unique in railway history. In her husband's time there were no buses at Slinfold and everybody went by train. There was a flourishing goods trade in those days and Mrs. Garman made the interesting observation that they used to have a lot more goods traffic than passengers on the Guildford-Horsham line. At Christmas the parcel traffic used to increase to such an extent that it was not uncommon for the parcels to reach the ceiling. To give you an idea of the vast dimensions of the goods in those early days, Mrs. Garman remembers five or six goods trains daily, whereas today there is only one. The railway made trade, speeded the mail and improved conditions. In its heyday it raised the social and economic conditions prevailing on the Surrey and North-West Sussex border.

Excursion trains especially were packed and Mrs. Garman remembers Slinfold Station so full on such occasions that the porters had great difficulty in making their way to the signal box. Speculation was rife, and local landowners were offered fantastic prices for their land. A hotel was built with grandiose schemes of developing it into the "Grosvenor" of rural Sussex. The licence has long been in abeyance, but the building, now a private residence, still stands as a reminder of those boom days which Mrs. Garman can so vividly recall. Although partially crippled with rheumatism and suffering from a somewhat hazy vision, Mrs. Garman is mentally alert, and with a face that would not disgrace a much younger lady. Her life has been the railway and although her 11 children (10 living), 25 grandchildren, and 23 great-grandchildren are the "apples" of her eye, memory ever holds the door and she travels the sweet lanes of reminiscence, which all eventually become interlinked with Slinfold Station and the Horsham-Guildford line. The years swing back. We see a crowded station, the stationmaster, his top hat gleaming in the sunshine, sports a magnificent carnation as he presides with benign efficiency over a staff of four. A blaze of colour greets the eye and we are attracted by the neat appearance of flower beds and lawn which betray the presence of "green fingers". The vision fades and we are at South View Cottage, Park Street, Slinfold, listening to a venerable old lady who has witnessed the making of railway history.

Resuming my railway journey I was soon transported the necessary two-and-a-quarter miles to Rudgwick. Our way lay through large tree-lined fields of vivid hue. The River Arun wound with placid tranquillity beneath us entirely unruffled at the thought of joining the sea. The heavy morning mist began to lift and as we drew into Rudgwick Station the sun beamed benevolently down.

Rudgwick is another single platform station, straggling beside this lone track. Regular Porter Jack Tetley, Relief Signalman Alec Shore and Learner Arthur Wood are the virtual lords of this domain and extremely hospitable fellows I found them. It is a cosy little station nestling in a hollow between Rudgwick and Bucks Green. One of this district's most interesting exports is mushrooms. Mr. Kirk, of Sheaves Farm, Loxwood, is one of England's foremost exponents in the art of mushroom cultivation. He sends an average of 90 chip baskets a day to Covent Garden via Rudgwick Station and has already sent mushroom spawn by air as far as Geneva. As Loxwood is a village some four miles to the west of Rudgwick I was unable to confirm how many people were employed in this flourishing little industry, however local people estimated Mr. Kirk's staff at approximately eight men and three women packers. Until recently Mr. Kirk ordered a hundred tons of manure from Covent Garden twice or three times a year, but he had been unable to get a regular supply lately to the detriment of the railway as his new supplies are delivered by road. Rudgwick is making great strides in the mushroom world, for in the village itself Mr. Boothman has just founded another mushroom farm, which already is dispatching approximately 32 chip basketsfull a day. The cultivation of mushrooms is an interesting study. They are grown in dark sheds which has the effect of forcing the spawn to develop much quicker than their poor cousins of the fields. The fresh, lump manure is turned approximately three times to gain the right temperature, and then sprayed with a chemical solution by men wearing masks. I gathered that a moist atmosphere, an even temperature, and good spawn are the three golden rules for indoor mushroom cultivation. As the indoor mushroom season never ends it would not surprise me if, in years to come, Rudgwick, with two progressive farms already established, became one of Britain's leading mushroom centres.

There are a number of market-gardeners in the vicinity of Rudgwick, including one who sends plants as far north as Carlisle, Wakefield and Manchester. An enterprising farmer sends bales of straw bi-monthly during the winter season to the Channel Islands, whilst until this autumn the nearby Ellens Green Racing Stables provided the inmates for four or five horse boxes a month. Of the other goods dealt with at Rudgwick Station, coal tops the list followed, not necessarily in this order, by agricultural seed, potatoes, and similar commodities.

The parcel traffic is quite good but although the average passenger traffic more than doubles that of Slinfold, it is by no means satisfactory. The dearth of trains is, of course, a serious handicap, but the canny folk of Rudgwick and Bucks Green seem more concerned with the cost. In 1939 they were able to travel excursion rate to Littlehampton for half-a-crown, today a cheap day return even to Horsham costs 1s. 6d. Meanwhile the bus fares remain more or less stationary at 1s. 2d. for a monthly return to Horsham. A cheap day ticket to Guildford would be a popular innovation.

Although the station buildings at Rudgwick were completed in time for the opening of the line on October 2, 1865, it was not until some months later that it was officially commissioned as a passenger station. The Board of Trade raised a strong objection to the unusually steep gradient of 1 in 80 on which the station was built. They also raised one or two minor queries relating to incompleteness of work but these were soon cleared up to everybody's satisfaction. With regard to the gradient, however, the Board of Trade stood firm and insisted that the embankments be altered to allow the track to run parallel with the platform at a reduced gradient of 1 in 130. Upon the completion of this work, Rudgwick Station took its rightful place on the Horsham-Guildford line. It is interesting to note that even as late as 1939 the "Up" excursion trains ignored Rudgwick, only coming to a halt at Baynards, one-and-a-quarter miles along the line. Could it be that the gradient is still considered unsafe for crowded passenger trains? In days gone by Rudgwick goods yard was a hive of industry. So much so in fact that the Company had to put a restriction on the goods traffic entering the yard. To ease the strain it was decided to purchase a nearby meadow where it was planned to build a model goods yard worthy of the traffic. In the meantime, however, the goods traffic slumped to more reasonable proportions and the new goods yard was rightly considered an unnecessary luxury. The meadow still serves to remind us of those "good old days" when Rudgwick Station was served by a station master, two signalmen, two porters, and a clerk.

Rudgwick's last station master went to Baynards Station in the mid-1920s, from which base he administered the needs of both stations. Although it is perched in the north-west corner of the county, Rudgwick is essentially a Sussex village. Etymologists translate the name Rudgwick as "the hill-side abode" and if we in turn make this plural, the

'Take 1' (perhaps!). M7 No 30026, disguised not very convincingly as No 26 at Baynards Station, taking a leading role during filming for BBC TV's Children's Hour series 'The Railway Children'. Sunday, 17 February 1957. *Bluebell Railway Museum*

description is apt today. I went on a circular tour from the station, bearing left up the hill to the church, which shows some Early English (13th century) features, particularly in the tower. Mr. E. V. Lucas describes it as "the most comfortable-looking church tower in Sussex", and although I do not pretend to have seen anything like all the church towers in Sussex, I am more than prepared to take his word for it. Certainly, Rudgwick Church is one of the shyest in the county. It does not even relax behind a mass of foliage, nothing less than the solid bulk of a local inn and general shop will do. But if you are interested in rural churches, wander up the narrow alley and if you are genuinely interested it will be worth your while. Taking the first road to the left (clearly sign-posted as Lynwick Street), I wandered by a cottage and farm to Bucks Green where, ignoring the temptation to turn right in search of renowned view-points, I forked left and then first left again until I arrived back at the station. In passing I must mention Mr. Atkinson and his Shetland ponies. I gather that at a recent show in Cardiff, Mr. Atkinson's ponies brought home the prizes in every available class.

After this commendable performance, you will not be surprised that some of his ponies have left Rudgwick Station bound for places as far afield as Norway and Australia. Soon after leaving Rudgwick Station our train forsakes the wholesome beauty of the countryside for the 381 yards of Baynards Tunnel. Whereupon emerging somewhat dazed from its restricted confines, we find that Sussex has receded and we are now in Surrey, or perhaps it would be more pertinent to say that we pass from the jurisdiction of Station Master Bonny of Christ's Hospital into that of Station Master Goodsell, of Cranleigh.

At first sight Baynards Station reminded me of the late Will Hay and his railway satires. As it happened my first impressions were confirmed by Signalman Maurice Scrace, who informed me that Baynards Station had been featured in two films, including one of the inimitable Will

A more tranquil Baynards. Like so many stations with a passing loop on what was otherwise a single line railway; potentially 10 minutes of feverish activity when two trains might cross but otherwise a couple of hours of slumber...
John Bailey

Hay entitled "The Black Sheep of Whitehall". It appears that Will, gorgeously attired in female garb, got helplessly mixed up in an invalid chair at the level crossing as the local express cantered by. Although I did not actually see the film, one can readily imagine the comical possibilities of such a scene especially when it starred so versatile an artist as Will Hay.

The other film appearance of Baynards Station was in "They were Sisters", another British film which was shot on a Sunday. This was really only a stooge part as the scene was the everyday one of a train's arrival and departure. Maurice saw the latter being filmed and was astounded at the time it took to bring this seemingly easy little scene into its true perspective. It appears that railwaymen are not the only ones with a stony furrow to plough!

Joking apart Baynards Station is a perfect little goldmine to the Railway. It only employs a staff of two, Maurice Scrace and Gordon Charman, who apart from doing all the usual station and signal box routine, co-ordinate the two staff systems. Baynards is the first passing place west of Christ's Hospital and over this intermediate section the staff and ticket system is in operation. From here to Peasmarsh (Junction Signal Box) the electric train staff is used. But I am drifting from my explanation as to why Baynards Station is of such inestimable value to the Railway Company.

The bulk of my argument rests with Fullers Earth which Station Master Goodsell of Cranleigh estimates at being worth approximately £10,000 per annum to the Railway. An average of 90 trucks containing bulk sulphur arrives every three months from Deptford Wharf. Luckily for the station staff, however, the Fullers Earth employees unload their own supplies. It is a wonderful turnover for such an isolated little place. Another important commodity dealt with at Baynards Station is milk. I was not particularly surprised

...and it was during these otherwise quiet times that a man might well turn his hand to other activities. The gardens at Baynards a joy to behold. Not surprisingly the station won several prizes in the Station Gardens Competitions. ***Ian Hemhill / Transport Treasury***

at this although the yearly export figure of 23,000 gallons, all from Mr. MacAndrews of Pallinghurst Farm, was certainly rather startling. When one considers the meagre population of the district, its passenger receipts cannot be grumbled at. But in any case Baynards Station can be more than content to rest on its goods traffic laurels. Baynards level crossing, which lies to the east of the station, opens out into a magnificent fir lined road which leads ultimately to Lord Ennisdale's Baynards House.

The original Baynards House was built by William of Baynards who came over from Normandy with William the Conqueror. Amongst its many distinguished visitors may be mentioned King John of Magna Charta fame who utilised the house as a hunting lodge when residing at Guildford Castle. As the years passed by, its long gallery became the venue for the annual cricket match between the Sussex men of Rudgwick and the Surrey men of Cranleigh. Mr. Thurlow, a brother of Lord Thurlow, lived at Baynards House in the mid-19th century and it was he who sold this section of the land to the old Horsham and Guildford Direct Railway Company. Amongst the clauses Mr. Thurlow attached to his land agreement with the Railway Company was one that made the Company responsible for running a through carriage from Baynards to London each weekday. Not until Baynards House was sold to a gentleman with a Rolls-Royce, which took him direct to Guildford in time to connect with the main line trains, did the master of the manor forfeit his right to a through London carriage.

Previously the owner of Baynards House travelled up to town in the morning and back again in the evening with more style, although less speed, than his more modern successors. Another interesting clause connected with this

One of several 'last trains' over the line before closure. This particular excursion was the joint RCTS/LCGB 'Midhurst Belle' tour of 18 October 1964 which included No 30064 taking the service from Woking to Christ's Hospital. It is seen here passing Rudgwick – which goods yard and signal box / ground frame are now defunct. ***Gerald Daniels***

line is that in the land agreement between the late Colonel St. John, Squire of Slinfold, and the Railway Company whereby it was mutually agreed that Slinfold Station should under no circumstances whatsoever be closed to passenger traffic. By far the most distinctive building in the vicinity of Baynards Station is the Thurlow Arms, an inn with a thought for a past proprietor of the district. In the spring its garden ranges like a golden yellow shield towards the railway line. Wordsworth must have been thinking of just such a district as this when he wrote his ode to a daffodil. Go to Vachery in the season and your senses are confounded by "hosts of golden daffodils". Here is peace personified. Far from the madding crowds, this is rural England at her best.

It was with regret that I once more boarded our little train, bound this time for Cranleigh some three miles further up the line. As with practically all the settlements along this line Cranleigh surprised me. Firstly, it was much larger than I had expected and secondly it was not the anti-climax I had been gloomily promising myself ever since we had pulled out of Baynards Station. It is difficult to keep a tight rein on superlative adjectives when travelling the Horsham-Guildford line, but Cranleigh for its size is undoubtedly a gem. An old world air pervades the village and this is reflected in the shops and houses. A fine beech avenue enhances the main road west of the war memorial, giving it an atmosphere of rural simplicity. The church looks cool and dignified. The fantastic artistry of the sculptor has captured something more sincere than we are accustomed to find in a village fountain. That remarkable hospital bears more resemblance to an old-world teashop than a centre of healing. So one goes rambling on with unconnected verve, for Cranleigh is an individualistic village, and although the whole blends to a purpose which would make the average town planner green with envy, the mind's eye carries away individual pictures of confined areas. Perhaps it is because Cranleigh is too beautiful to survey in one sweeping glance? I wish I knew, for then I should understand the soul of Cranleigh. Cranleigh people are justly proud of their village which they claim to be the largest in England. They also claim to have a cricket pitch the size of the Oval. In fact they good-naturedly boast of many things including Cranleigh School which occupies a noteworthy position in the realms of education. Cranleigh School has very strong associations with its local railway station. Indeed I was told that but for the railway, Cranleigh School might never have existed. Be that as it may it is an authenticated fact that Cranleigh School was built in 1865 and officially opened within two

Leaving Baynards Tunnel in pull-push mode towards Rudgwick.

SLINFOLD

BRITISH RAILWAYS
SLINFOLD

months of the inaugural train service. In those early days the School owed much to the munificent help of the late Lord Ashcombe who piloted them through many a stormy patch. Today, however, under the wise Headmastership of the Rev. Loveday it is freely regarded as a fine example of the English Public School system. School holidays provide a headache for the Station staff, dispatching what Station Master Goodsell estimates as approximately 4-500 pieces of luggage. As at Christ's Hospital, the relationship between school and station is extremely cordial and by mutual co-operation "operation holiday" is efficiently completed to everybody's satisfaction. It may be claimed with some degree of confidence that the coming of the railway contributed to a greater or lesser extent in the development of Cranleigh.

Let us poach the recollections of one of Cranleigh's longest established tradesmen as he describes the social revolution the railway brought in its stead: "The coming of the Railway altered the whole outlook of the community. The youths discarded their smock frocks and the maidens their spriggy printed Manchester gowns. The postal service was also brought up to date. There had only been a daily post from Guildford which was brought in a small cart drawn by two mastiffs. Even this was a great advance on the previous system when the letters were brought once a week in two rush baskets by an old lady". Today the railway brings to Cranleigh something like 30 bags of mail daily. Such is progress!

Cranleigh is a popular weekend resort for the tourist but I regret to say that few of this much wooed fraternity travel by rail, using instead a bus to the village from Guildford station. Ewhurst, a fascinating community under the shadow of Pitch Hill, is only two or three miles distant by road, but by cultivating the acquaintance of this district's delightful lanes and footpaths, one may enjoy a good ramble. If upon arrival at Ewhurst you decide to call it a day, a half-hourly Saturday afternoon, or hourly Sunday bus service, will speedily return you safely to Cranleigh Station. Years ago there was a proposal to build a railway line from Ockley Station through Ockley village and Ewhurst to Cranleigh. I was unable to glean more information regarding this dream line but it does appear at the time of its conception to have been a concrete proposition. The staff of the Horsham and Guildford line impressed me by the keen and virile way they set about their work. Almost without exception they showed a zealous interest in the ways and means of increasing traffic over the line. Thus I was not surprised to discover in Station Master Goodsell of Cranleigh a man who had much to do with getting excursion tickets to London, Surbiton and Hampton Court introduced on to this line. Apart from Cranleigh he is responsible for Baynards and Bramley stations, both of which he visits daily. Although he has only been Station Master at Cranleigh for the past two years, Mr. Goodsell can claim more than a passing connection with this area having in the course of his service been clerk at both Bramley and Baynards.

Cranleigh enjoys an assorted goods traffic which justifies the employment of this line's only goods porter. Amongst the more interesting commodities dealt with, we may mention 25-30 baskets of mushrooms daily, several crates of lettuce in the season and various other market garden produce. On the import side 'Grimsby' is well represented with an average of 3½ tons of fish per week. Indeed it would be difficult to find anything Cranleigh does not deal with. An average of 1,100 passenger tickets are issued each month but Cranleigh is more proud of its 50 or so season ticket holders, an astoundingly high percentage of whom travel first class. Practically all these first class regulars travel up to town on the 8.24 a.m. train which by connecting with the main line electrics at

Opposite top: Basic railway status also at Slinfold; the yard crane and loading gauge now forever redundant. ***Gerald Daniels***

Opposite bottom: Rural accommodation; railway and family. ***Gerald Daniels*** **(Here might also be an appropriate place to mention the spelling error that appeared in Part 1 of this article, page 70 of ST3. The word 'arterioles' should read 'articles'. Sorry, slip of the finger [and the spell checker]. Many thanks to Denis Calvert for pointing it out.)**

Guildford manages to transport them to Waterloo by 9.30 a.m. This 8.24 a.m. from Cranleigh is therefore Station Master Goodsell's daily headache. For if the 8.24 a.m. happens to miss the connection at Guildford both the Divisional Superintendent at Redhill and Station Master Goodsell of Cranleigh hear all about it!

Ted Wright has been a ganger on the Cranleigh link for about 37 years and so when he retired recently his colleagues clubbed together for a farewell gift. The idea, as Station Master Goodsell put it at the presentation ceremony, was "to show in a tangible form our appreciation of his kindness and ever willing nature to all whom he came in contact". And so on this happy note another grand old stalwart of the line marked his official retirement from the service.

Cranleigh is unusually interesting and this even extends to its station which I regret to having treated in somewhat cavalier a fashion. The truth is of course that Cranleigh deserves a book and having half sidled from its intriguing tentacles I made a dash over the bridge and so on to the Bramley train.

Bramley, a rapidly expanding residential centre lying within easy reach of the hills, is five miles distant from Cranleigh and only three and a half from Guildford. It is therefore not surprising that the modern Bramley wears a rather suburban air and wears it very well too. But after the fresh character of its kindred settlements of the Horsham-Guildford line it was all so different and I simply was not in the mood to appreciate the change. At all events I could appreciate the neighbouring countryside which is ideal for ramblers. Bramley Station is handicapped by a frequent bus service to Guildford and there seems little hope of the railway regaining lost traffic here. There are however 25-30 season ticket holders, amongst them half a dozen first class. Yet the railway was once the sole public means of transport to and from Bramley. People walked miles to the station in those days and Station Master Goodsell of Cranleigh, who was once a booking clerk here, remembers issuing a hundred tickets for one train. Today Bramley's only serious traffic is the parcel service which is in a flourishing condition. The export of charcoal to the I.C.I. in Yorkshire has just started and it is to be hoped this will develop into a regular traffic. By this time I had become accustomed to discovering a famous school in the vicinity of most stations along this line. Bramley was no exception to this rule for here is situated St. Catherines Girls School and at holiday time the station deals with 80-100 pieces of luggage which require transportation to Jersey, Guernsey and other far away places. The "special" porter who, with the assistance of two signalmen, runs Bramley Station said that before the war girls used to be attracted to St. Catherines from abroad, but he does not think there are any foreigners there these days.

And so I set out from Bramley on the last stage of my journey. At Peasmarsh Junction signal box we merged into the main line and soon arrived at Guildford, the ancient capital of Surrey. The Town Council of Guildford have published the most de luxe Town Guide it has been my privilege to see. Tastefully bound in blue and gold it would enhance any bookcase and if a brief perusal of its pages does not convince you that Guildford is the place to reside or visit nothing else ever will. A charming town with an intriguing history, Guildford is too vast a subject to squeeze within the limited scope of this article. In any case towns were not for me that day, the call of the Horsham-Guildford line was too strong for that, and so, rejoining the little train, together we retraced our way over the border to Horsham, flower bedecked capital of North-West Sussex.

We passed through the same glorious country which had so endeared itself to me on the outward trip. Bramley, Cranleigh, Baynards, Rudgwick, Slinford and Christ's Hospital, these names really meant something now. As we drew into Horsham Station, my undivided attention was drawn to our little engine, whose astonishing feats of endurance had made this experience possible. It looked rather forlorn as it stood shorn of its natural background in this busy main line station. But withal one noticed a subtle streak of dignity which raised it somewhat from the common herd. Perhaps it was because I had come to understand this little engine whose strict observance to the timetable was only less surprising than it was commendable. I even stooped to make a note of its number, 2384, and Class E3.

Bill Edwards and Tom Brackpool, No. 2384's crew, were most enthusiastic about their charge and I was privileged to watch it taking a refreshing draught further down the platform. Leaving No. 2384 to its memories I rushed over the bridge in time to see one of the rarities of the Southern Region pull its load out of the station en route for Guildford. Mr. V. H. Nelson of Malmesbury, Wilts., who appealed in the Magazine recently for the preservation of at least one of this class, would have been especially pleased to see it. For the engine was none other than a class D1 tank, No. 2252. As this veteran of the railroad raced with the agility of youth for Guildford, I experienced pangs of regret that I should not be accompanying him. For with regard to the Horsham-Guildford line I feel inclined to agree with Robert Louis Stevenson "that it is better to travel than to arrive".

Back to the hustle and bustle of the main line at Guildford. It was here that branch trains from Christ's Hospital would terminate or commence, surrounded by the swish electrics to and from Portsmouth, the cross-country services between Reading and Redhill, services to Aldershot, and the 'new-line' trains to Waterloo. Some of these might well be electric workings but there was also steam, such as this S15 no doubt about to create a dust storm as it passes through the station platforms with ballast from far off Meldon.

Southern Allocations - Eastern Section 1934 Part 3: Reading, Redhill, St Leonards and Tonbridge

Reading							
1025	F1	4-4-0		1225	C	0-6-0	
1042	F1	4-4-0		1658	R	0-4-4T	Motor Train fitted
1047	R1	0-6-0T		1659	R	0-4-4T	Motor Train fitted
1056	F1	4-4-0		1662	R	0-4-4T	Motor Train fitted
1074	F1	4-4-0		1666	R	0-4-4T	Motor Train fitted
1117	F1	4-4-0		1667	R	0-4-4T	Motor Train fitted
1118	F1	4-4-0		1672	R	0-4-4T	Motor Train fitted
1143	F1	4-4-0		1708	R1	0-6-0T	Motor Train fitted
1174	R1	0-6-0T		1709	R1	0-6-0T	Motor Train fitted
1187	F1	4-4-0		1861	N	2-6-0	
1202	F1	4-4-0					

Seen from a slightly different angle, this is Reading SR shed from the perspective of the GW lines. Former SECR 'D' class 4-4-0 No 31577 is standing outside the depot on 2 May 1956. 4-4-0s were a common sight at Reading for many years and whilst the F1 class had by the 1950s been superseded here, others of similar wheel arrangement would serve here until they too were ousted by Moguls and later BR Standard types. ***A. E. Bennett / Transport Treasury***

Redhill											
1028	F1	4-4-0		1234	C	0-6-0		1523	H	0-4-4T
1030	F1	4-4-0		1260	C	0-6-0		1636	U	2-6-0
1035	F1	4-4-0		1262	C	0-6-0		1637	U	2-6-0
1041	O1	0-6-0		1267	C	0-6-0		1723	C	0-6-0
1109	O1	0-6-0		1279	H	0-4-4T		1725	C	0-6-0
1152	R	0-4-4T		1293	C	0-6-0		1801	U	2-6-0
1182	H	0-4-4T		1425	O1	0-6-0		1802	U	2-6-0
1185	F1	4-4-0		1429	O1	0-6-0		1804	U	2-6-0
1193	H	0-4-4T		1480	C	0-6-0		1824	N	2-6-0
1216	F1	4-4-0								

We view Redhill from a passing train taking the route east to Tonbridge. Redhill shed had been rebuilt in the form seen in 1925 and continued to be a service and stabling point for steam until 1965. In its later years it also became a collecting ground for withdrawn and stored locos. To the right of the coaling stage – see rising on higher ground – was the main line to Brighton, whilst the Quarry line also emerged from a tunnel near the rear of the site. Two engines were identified by the photographer as his train passed, Nos 32349 (K class) and U 31797. ***Ken Coursey / Transport Treasury***

St Leonards								
903	V	4-4-0	*Charterhouse*		1215	F1	4-4-0	
904	V	4-4-0	*Lancing*		1228	F1	4-4-0	
905	V	4-4-0	*Tonbridge*		1249	F1	4-4-0	
906	V	4-4-0	*Sherborne*		1335	R1	0-6-0T	
907	V	4-4-0	*Dulwich*		1339	R1	0-6-0T	
908	V	4-4-0	*Westminster*		1760	L	4-4-0	
909	V	4-4-0	*St Paul's*		1761	L	4-4-0	
913	V	4-4-0	*Christ's Hospital*		1762	L	4-4-0	
914	V	4-4-0	*Eastbourne*		1763	L	4-4-0	
915	V	4-4-0	*Brighton*		1764	L	4-4-0	
1060	F1	4-4-0			1765	L	4-4-0	
1079	F1	4-4-0			1766	L	4-4-0	
1097	F1	4-4-0			2364	D3	0-4-4T	Motor Train fitted
1088	F1	4-4-0			2367	D3	0-4-4T	Motor Train fitted
1094	F1	4-4-0			2368	D3	0-4-4T	Motor Train fitted
1156	F1	4-4-0			2390	D3	0-4-4T	Motor Train fitted
1192	F1	4-4-0			2394	D3	0-4-4T	Motor Train fitted
1196	F1	4-4-0			2522	C2X	0-6-0	
1199	F1	4-4-0			2538	C2X	0-6-0	
1208	F1	4-4-0						

Four locos at St. Leonards and with others on shed in the background, 26 August 1956. Note the ground disc signal in the 'off' position for an engine to come out of the shed. Of those seen, only the first is positively identified, R1 No 31174. Behind this is a 'Terrier', next an H class 0-4-4T and finally a 'Schools'. Engines of the latter class were based here from the time of their introduction and worked the London express services until superseded in the late 1950s by the 'Hastings' DEMU sets. ***A. E. Bennett / Transport Treasury***

Tonbridge										
1013	B1	4-4-0		1227	C	0-6-0		1451	B1	4-4-0
1021	B1	4-4-0		1229	C	0-6-0		1512	H	0-4-4T
1048	O1	0-6-0		1252	C	0-6-0		1553	H	0-4-4T
1054	C	0-6-0		1253	C	0-6-0		1577	D	4-4-0
1057	D	4-4-0		1257	C	0-6-0		1586	D	4-4-0
1059	C	0-6-0		1305	H	0-4-4T		1591	D	4-4-0
1064	O1	0-6-0		1309	H	0-4-4T		1730	D	4-4-0
1066	O1	0-6-0		1320	H	0-4-4T		1733	D	4-4-0
1084	F1	4-4-0		1324	H	0-4-4T		1734	D	4-4-0
1086	C	0-6-0		1432	O1	0-6-0		1737	D	4-4-0
1110	F1	4-4-0		1437	O1	0-6-0		1738	D	4-4-0
1123	O1	0-6-0		1439	O1	0-6-0		1746	D	4-4-0
1150	C	0-6-0		1441	B1	4-4-0		1748	D	4-4-0
1204	F1	4-4-0		1443	B1	4-4-0		1750	D	4-4-0
1206	F1	4-4-0		1444	B1	4-4-0		2234	D1	0-4-2
1212	F1	4-4-0		1450	B1	4-4-0		2358	D1	0-4-2
1219	C	0-6-0								

C2X No 32443 in early BR guise outside Tonbridge shed – the Q1s behind were common bedfellows here from 1942 onwards. Steam was of course the dominant motive power in the area until the Kent Electrification and in consequence the allocation was around the 50 engines mark in the 1930s but had risen to 64 immediately prior to nationalisation. This was probably its peak and numbers dwindled, associated with changing traffic patterns, until closure around the Winter of 1962/63. *Transport Treasury*

John Davenport

A lifelong railway interest - and some official footplate trips.

Part 1: Wartime and beyond

In 2021 the railway hobby lost one of its senior enthusiasts, John Davenport. John had been a committed steam enthusiast throughout his lifetime, in later years becoming well known among that group of individuals who supported the Merchant Navy Locomotive Preservation Society and No 35028 *Clan Line.*

I had the privilege of meeting John some years ago, he was of quiet disposition, extremely polite but once one got to know him underneath there was a wealth of stories and recollections. Over time John had also amassed a veritably treasure trove of princely relics, nameplates galore and I was allowed to see only on the condition I agreed to an undertaking I would not divulge his identity or location. (John moved house a few years later whilst the collection has also since been disposed of.)

Subsequent to his passing I was privileged to receive a call from Mrs Wendy Davenport asking if I would like custody of some of John's papers, including his written notes. It was fascinating to read these and in consequence this is the start of a short series featuring John's railway recollections accompanied by some of his photographs - most of the latter are held in the archives at the Transport Treasury.

In John's words, 'I became a train spotter in April 1942. I have no idea what started me writing down engine numbers at that time. We had lived in a house on the high ground to the west of Woking since December 1933, between the Portsmouth and Southampton lines. The former was nearer but at the bottom of a steep hill, and as traffic was almost totally electric by 1942, the Southampton line was preferred. Helpfully the bike ride to St Johns Hill Road overbridge was almost level, due to the depth of the Goldsworth Hill cutting. Another spotting site was the Tin Bridges, which crossed both lines just to the west of Woking Junction.

'My father was a peacetime commuter from Woking. Sometime in late 1939 he was told he would be appointed, along with some of his City colleagues, as a Temporary Civil Servant in the Ministry of Supply, and that would be his wartime occupation. So he continued to commute (the travels of Blitz journeys are another story), and became known to Mr Avery, the Woking Station Master. What follows are two pieces of family lore, although they pre-date my train spotting. The first was included in "Return from Dunkirk" by Peter Tatlow (Oakwood Press 2002).

'Somehow it was discovered that Father could speak French, so when French troops evacuated from Dunkirk were being repatriated via West Country ports, he was asked by Mr Avery to bring any of his friends who could speak French to the station. Along with the W.V.S. and other organisations, he found himself handing out cups of tea and words of encouragement. The trains had come via Redhill and Guildford, and were reversing direction at Woking to head west.

'The second dates to around March 1941. Father was the Chief A.R.P. Warden of the western part of Hook Heath. One night when there were German planes about, he was on patrol. At the crossroads at the edge of the escarpment overlooking Guildford he met some of the local Home Guard. While they were there, someone noticed a flashing green light away to the south. There did not seem to be a regular pattern of flashes, but it was highly suspicious. Fortunately one of the party had a compass and various bearings were taken.

'As this seemed to be a military matter, it was left to the Home Guard to take further. It was reported next day that the posse had not discovered a nest of spies, rather that it had found one of Worplesdon's Down automatic colour light signals. Even with the projecting hood on the signal head the light had been visible at some distance, and the intermittent flashing had been caused by branches in the

As will be gathered from the text, John was an avid enthusiast throughout his life. This included wielding a camera wherever possible, such as at Woking in May 1960 where he recorded S15 No 30506 putting up a smokescreen as it battles away with the heavy 10.45 am Feltham to Salisbury freight. ***John Davenport / Transport Treasury***

line of sight moving in the wind. That was the family spy story.

'Returning to the more important theme of train spotting, there was a great shortage of information. Ian Allan's first Southern ABC appeared in December 1942, so recording names and numbers was totally haphazard. Fortunately a change encounter on the railway bridge rescued me. My Deputy Headmaster, Gerald Cannon, was a serious enthusiast and gave me one of his old Southern stockbooks. I also discovered there were two other older railway fans in the school.

'The relationship between Mr Avery, the Woking Station Master, and my father got us an invitation to the signal box. Resulting from the 1937 rebuilding and the installation of colour light signalling, it was fascinating. No great crashing levers – it was more like a model railway in operation. The track diagram showed the progress of trains in red lights, while each miniature signal lever had coloured lights above it to show the aspect displayed. There were two signalmen on duty, one at each end of the frame. We were allowed to operate some levers, under strict supervision. There was enough traffic to be interesting.

'Some time in 1943, the three of us from school were asked through Mr Avery whether we would like to visit Feltham marshalling yard. Not surprisingly, the answer was yes, so we set off via Weybridge and Virginia Water. On arrival we were given an explanatory talk on how the yard worked and then taken to the signal box controlling one of the humps. The operating system was a mixture of basic procedures and contemporary technology. The signalman had a horizontal track diagram with two push buttons for the control of each set of

A visit to Basingstoke saw him record 700 class No 30368 stored next to the buffers with one of the vehicles of the breakdown train behind. No date was given. ***John Davenport / Transport Treasury***

points. The string of wagons pushed up the hump by the G16 4-8-0 tank was split into units for each siding by shunters. The number of each required siding was chalked on the end of the front wagon, often on the buffer head. The signalman had to read the numbers and set the appropriate points with little time to spare between each set. It was much too quick for the amateurs and I think we caused the odd miss-sort.

'It was now time to eat our sandwiches, and we were shown into a meeting room to do this. Afterwards we were hoisted on to the footplate of the G16s and given a tour of the yard. We finished by pushing a long train over one of the humps. For a first footplate ride this was most impressive. The power of the locomotive was very apparent with the effort on the fire of each piston stroke as we made steady progress. The general noise was terrific.

'Everyone we met was friendly and helpful, and obviously our day had been carefully planned. On the way home we were discussing this when one of the party said that while we having lunch he had heard two railwaymen talking. From what they said, it was believed we had come from the Southern Railway Orphanage at Woking – hence the red carpet treatment.

'The usual base for train spotting was Tin Bridges. Situated immediately to the west of Woking Junction, it crossed all the lines starting with the Down goods shunting and reception tracks and the Portsmouth Down and Up lines, there was about a hundred yards of cinder road to the bridge over the four Southampton tracks. This was a massive piece of LSWR engineering with high plate sides. Next to this, at a slight angle, was a newer span with concrete floor and criss-cross girder sides. This spanned the two Up goods reception roads.

'The greater visibility was obtained from the brick abutments on the Down side of the

Opposite: John was privileged to have several official footplate trips on the SR main line and, being official trips, this meant he would be accompanied by a Loco Inspector. Here we see Driver Billins and Inspector Danny Knight at the time John rode No 35004 *Cunard White Star* from Exeter to Salisbury. (More footplate views and crews in the second instalment in Issue 5.)

SPECIAL NOTICE
GARLIC
HOT INSIDE BIG-END

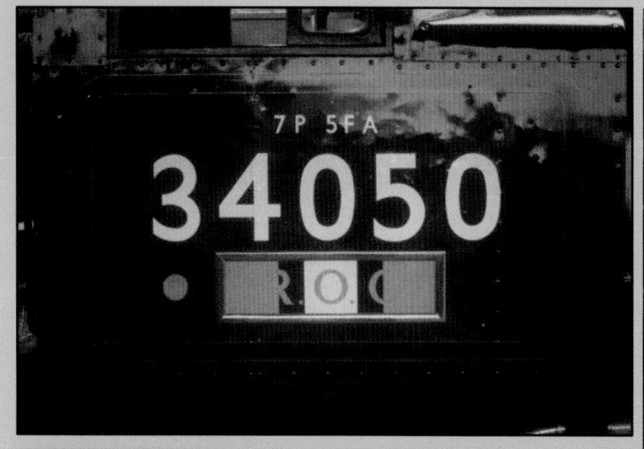

This page and opposite: John was a member and later supporter of the 'Royal Observer Corps' throughout his life and especially when No 34050, bearing the same name, was awarded its 'Long Service' ribbon (12 years continuous service) at Waterloo on 2 July 1961. The 'bulled-up' engine is seen together with the Commandant of the Corps performing the ceremony. John had a wry smile when he recalled the occasion, '...I was a mere 'irk' and would normally never have got anywhere near, but I knew Waterloo and by dodging around a bit I was able to come out past the engine further up the platform without being seen. Hence I was able to get my photographs...'

Southampton line. After the publication of the Southern Electric ABC it became important to view the Portsmouth traffic more closely. In mitigation of this behaviour, we had pretty well run out of steam cops by then.

'Beyond the goods loops were considerable sidings. At the northern edge, the Permanent Way Department had its depot. This was operated by a self-propelled steam crane, which never came into clear view but was of antique appearance. The external cladding seemed to be dilapidated corrugated iron sheets. Movement was quick with a distinctive chuffing exhaust.

'The Down side shunter was one of Guildford's M7s, frequently No 22 or 26. The Up side usually had No 349, a G6 from the same shed. There was not much traffic between the Up and Down goods yards. Infrequently the Up side shunter would propel a rake of wagons and no brake van, but with a tail lamp hung on the last wagon, energetically across the main line and into the Down yard. I do not remember an opposite working.

'In 1942, before the Merchant Navy class became regulars, the main line services through Woking were worked by Lord Nelsons, King Arthurs, and Schools, with H15 and T14 classes on secondary services and van trains. The Feltham goods were in the hands of Urie S15s. The 3.30pm Waterloo to Bournemouth was known as the four o'clock Schools. The larger Drummond 4-4-0s were also around. By March 1944 I had seen all but one L12 and all but two D15s, but they have not left any lasting impression. The Maunsell moguls were represented by the U class. The H16 4-6-2Ts

based at Feltham were regular performers on the Feltham – Guildford freights, with the exception of No 520 which never seemed to appear.

'Various Western Section engines were lent to other railways to fill shortages, such as the N15X 'Remembrance' and some N15s and S15s. In exchange, and because after Dunkirk there was less traffic in Kent and Sussex, we received a collection of replacements. The most effective were the Maunsell D1 and E1 4-4-0 rebuilds of which I can remember Nos 1019,1145,1247,1492 and 1494. They had a very distinctive and purposeful exhaust beat. Less effective were the B4X 4-4-0s, including Nos 2043,2072 and 2073. All these 4-4-0s worked on the Basingstoke and beyond stopping trains.

'More exotic visitors were the H2 Brighton Atlantics. Transferred to Basingstoke they worked the business semi-fast but were apparently not popular because they did not appear as frequently after 1942. Much more exciting were the two big Brighton 4-6-2s, Nos 2325 and 2326. We were not used to large tank engines on passenger trains, so they did make a lasting impression.

'There were some elderly locomotives still working. The K10 and L11 4-4-0s seemed particularly aged and were usually seen on vans and goods. According to my ABC I saw No 666, an Adams X6 4-4-0. I believe it was on an Up pick-Up goods which must have been one of its last outings. Some other Adams classes were very sprightly; G6 No 349 has already been mentioned and one of the surviving A12 0-4-2s would appear on the Guildford – Woking livestock trains. The cattle trucks were then attached to a through service. The A12 moved its three or four trucks at quite a speed, and its appearance at Tin Bridges was greeted by shouts of 'The Piggeries'. I think our identification was incorrect. The 0395 0-6-0s were credible performers and the Guildford based ones were very familiar. Less aged and more powerful were the Drummond 700 class, which seemed to attract quite heavy loads.

'At the other end of the age range were the Merchant Navy Pacifics, the first ten of which appeared between 1941 and July 1942 and the second ten between December 1944 and June 1945. I suppose we must have seen some of the test runs with enormous loads. It was on their return from banishment to sort out the reliability problems that they made their impression, and the sent ten 'just appeared'. While the air-smoothed casing was different on the Southern, it was not so startling as we had photos of A4s in our books and the lineage was there if a little different, particularly at the front.'

Next time: Further wartime recollections and some further VIP visits.

We start The Townroe selection with this stunning 1955 portrait of T9 No 30719 on a special West of England duty recorded near Woking in 1955 with a Down inspection train. Built at Nine Elms in 1899, the engine had a life of 61 years until meeting its end in early 1961. The clean black livery goes well with the crimson and cream coaches, not a particularly onerous task for the engine, just two coaches, but possibly a special working that may be required to stop several times en-route.

Stephen Townroe's Colour Archive; Adams and Drummond Part 1

For the next two issues we will be concentrating on the designs of Messrs Adams and Drummond. In the 1950s there still remained examples of both at work; maybe not perhaps in their prime but still performing useful service. All would subsequently be swept away a few years later, replaced by more modern traction, both steam and diesel, or because services had been withdrawn on the lines they had previously worked upon.

Local freight on the erstwhile Meon Valley line 70 years ago. Another T9, this time No 30313, is near Soberton (Droxford) with a Down freight in 1953. As with many branch and cross country routes, this railway was built to double track standards although only a single line of rails was laid – notice the width of the underbridge. There has also been concern for track creep, as concrete derricks have been let into the ballast between the rails from which regular measurements might be taken to the running rail to determine movement. No 30313 had been built in 1901 but like the engine seen earlier was similarly taken out of service in 1961.

Top: B4 dock shunter No 30096, formerly named *Normandy*, being serviced inside Eastleigh shed on an unreported date. Alongside is a Maunsell Q, and beyond that possibly a Drummond 700. The diminutive size of these engines made them ideal for shunting on sharp curves, hence when replaced by more modern engines in the form of the USA class, they still found useful work acting as pilot engines at sheds or, as in the case with No 30096, shunting the tight curves in the goods yard at Winchester City. No 30096 remained in this role until the autumn of 1963 when it was replaced by a diesel but found further industrial use at Corrals in Southampton after which it was preserved.

Bottom: Another Adams loco was G6 0-6-0T No 30266, seen in the final stages of overhaul at Eastleigh in July 1954. At the time the engine was already 60 years old but still had a further six years ahead before final retirement. It appears as if the engine has just been re-wheeled with limited remaining work necessary; dome cover and couplings at least. No 30266 would be sent to Salisbury once work was complete and where it would remain for the rest of its service life.

Opposite: With SCT based at Eastleigh it is not surprising Eastleigh would feature in many of his images. This is the front of the shed in 1949, No 30726 just arrived back from the adjacent works after overhaul but as this is 1949 no emblem was yet ready to be applied to the tender. The lined 'mixed traffic' livery suited the class well – when kept clean at least. Between 1949 and withdrawal in 1959, the engine had a number of homes, being respectively at Eastleigh, Salisbury, Basingstoke, Fratton and finally Exmouth Junction.

30726
30726
SOUTHERN

Top: North of Eastleigh from the water meadows adjacent to the River Itchen and the Itchen navigation, we see an unidentified M7 on a Southampton to Alton train. The service is likely travelling on the nearest of the four tracks at this point, the Up slow, and will already have called at Northam, St Denys, Swaythling and Eastleigh. Still to come are Shawford, Winchester City, Itchen Abbas, Alresford, Ropley, Medstead & Four Marks, and finally Alton. All a bit of a mouthful at stations where a tannoy was provided.

Bottom: Another rural idyll, this time a pull-push working - with the engine leading - on the 'Old Road' between Lymington Junction and Holmesley. The service is probably a Brockenhurst_Poole, Brockenhurst – Bournemouth West train. The date is July 1953, the BR crest now in evidence on the tank sides and the coaches in standard maroon as used for branch line workings.

Opposite top: Possibly the same tran but recorded a bit earlier – the date is still the same, July 1953. This time we also know the engine, M7 No 30111, crossing from the Down main line on to the 'branch'. The tall stop signal on the right was the home signal for trains off the Lymington branch which also diverged at this point.

Opposite bottom: Another branch line / junction view, this time Winchester Junction and the train an Up Alton M7 pull – push service having just left the main line and, although out of sight, collecting the tablet for the single line section to Alresford. The main line disappears north towards Wallers Ask and Basingstoke whilst it was at this point Down main line trains might sometimes reach their maximum speeds on occasions in excess of the 85 mph line speed.

30047

Opposite top: 700 class 0-6-0 No 30315 returning to Eastleigh past Shawford Junction after attending to the 1960 derailment at Whitchurch Town. (No 76026 came off the line at the sand-drag protecting the single line.) The engine is in charge of the Salisbury breakdown crane and is taking the goods loop that will pass around the back of Shawford station on its way back to Salisbury via Eastleigh with the crane. This engine had a life of 65 years from 1879 and was one of the last of the class in service until December 1962. (Two cranes had been needed to deal with the accident, that from Eastleigh and also the Salisbury crane.)

Opposite bottom: Another branch line duty for an M7, this time in Sussex on the line between Petersfield and Pulborough via Midhurst. No 30047 is in propelling mode near Selham in April 1954, passenger services on this line having less than a year to survive. The engine was based at Horsham at the time and had been since 1949. It would remain here until moving to Brighton in July 1957 and from where it ceased work just seven months later in February 1960.

This page, top: A July 1951 view of Drummond S11 4-4-0 No 30403 and with its seemingly high pitched boiler. From the head code, the engine is on a Bournemouth West to Dorchester service (but returning to Bournemouth West) and was photographed passing Branksome shed. Notice the LMS 'Black 5' and also the 'Britannia' Pacific in the background. There is also a good comparison in the width of the carriage stock, the first vehicle being of Maunsell design and the remainder of the train a narrow LSWR '3-set'. This was the final year of service for No 30403, ten engines of the class 'on the books' at the start of the year but only one 12 months later. The final survivor going in 1954.

This page, centre: '0395' No 30566 in steam at Eastleigh in 1953 and according to SCT's notes, '...fitted with wooden Drummond snow-plough'. During the winter months it was practice for depots to fit an engine with a snow plough which was then kept in readiness for the winter. Note the attachment required the removal of the buffers and consequently the engine was incapable of other work whilst so fitted. No 30566 dated back to 1885 and was a useful and long lived engine in service until 1959.

This page bottom: We conclude with another pull-push service near Holmesley, this time in 1950 and clearly with the engine – no number – leading. This line, double track throughout, was a useful diversionary line avoiding Bournemouth. It was probably busiest on summer weekends when a succession of special and relief services would be routed this way. During the week some Waterloo workings would also use the line so crews might retain 'route knowledge'.

Next time, Part 2 of Adams and Drummond locos.

(Electronic copies of the SCT colour images are available for private and commercial use. Please contact the Editor directly.)

Steel Sleepers on the Southern Railway (Reproduced from 'The Railway Engineer', January 1929)

'Steel sleepers on the Southern Railway. Thirty-five miles of track are to be equipped with Sandberg steel sleepers for British Bull-Head track.

'Part of the proceedings of the Centenary Celebration of the Institution of Civil Engineers was a Conference on 5 June. One of the papers then read and discussed was by Mr. C. J. Brown, entitled "Developments in the Use of Materials in Railway Engineering." Two of the speakers were Mr. W. W. Grierson (GWR) and Mr. G. Ellson (SR), both of whom referred to the desirability of finding a substitute for wooden sleepers. Mr. Ellson, in his observations, remarked that the Southern Railway had had some pressed-steel sleepers in use on the London–Portsmouth main line for 7½ years, and that they were in perfect condition still, whilst the ganger said that they gave less trouble in maintenance than timber.

'That these results have been quite satisfactory is seen in the recent announcement that the Southern Railway has placed an order for 70,000, or 5,000 tons, of sleepers with a British firm of steel-makers - The United Steel Companies. These sleepers are not the usual steel sleeper, as used in India, South America and on the Continent, as that form is for the flat-bottom rail. What the Southern has been trying, and those now ordered, are for bull-headrail which needs a chair when the wooden sleeper is used. In the present case the jaws that hold the rail by the web are an integral part of the sleeper, and the only separate parts are the two baseplates and the two keys for each sleeper.'

Below we publish the official announcement issued by the Southern Railway regarding this matter: 'An initial order for 70,000 steel sleepers, equal to 5,000 tons of steel, has been placed by the Southern Railway with a British firm. The Southern, which was the first main-line company to install colour light signalling on a large scale in place of the semaphore signals, is thus the first British company to adopt the steel sleeper in preference to that made of timber.

'The supply ordered by the Southern Railway will enable about 35 miles of selected track to be equipped over a period of two years. Although this is not a great amount, it is the first step towards a new avenue of prosperity for the British steel industry, and as such the Southern Railway is glad to be able to take it.

'A ton of steel equals about 14 sleepers, and costs about £11, the sleeper complete costing about 15s. 6d. The 'chair' is integral (unlike the wooden sleeper, to which it must be separately fixed), and only the 'key' and two small plates remain to be provided. The price of timber sleepers has been increasing, due to shortage, and a further point in the present innovation is that all the most suitable timber is foreign. With the double view of avoiding the higher costs in future, and helping, if it could, a British industry badly in need of it, the Southern Railway has for some years past been making experiments with steel sleepers on the London - Portsmouth line, over which pass the heavy 'King Arthur' type locomotives, and the most modern rollingstock. The results having satisfied their technical experts, the directors have approved the first substantial order for steel sleepers, and money which has hitherto gone abroad will now stay in Britain.

'When it is remembered that the annual consumption of sleepers on railways in Great Britain is in the neighbourhood of 4,000,000, it will be seen that if only 10 per cent. of this total were steel sleepers it would mean an order to the British steel industry of about 30,000 tons of steel every year.

'At the present issue price of timber sleepers, with the necessary chairs and fastenings, and assuming an equal life of 20 years for the steel and timber article, the cost of installation and maintenance, including renewal, is about the same, but if the price of timber sleepers increased by only 6d. there would be a considerable saving in favour of the steel sleepers, not only in the initial outlay but in maintenance and renewal. It is, however, anticipated that the life of the steel sleeper will exceed that of the timber, and from experience gained in countries where steel has been used, there would seem to be every likelihood of this. In Germany it is estimated at 30 years. On the other hand, if steel sleepers become general in Britain, it is reasonable to assume that the price will go down, which will enable still further economies to be effected. We may add that the sleepers ordered have been increased in stiffness to the extent of 110 per cent. above that of the trial sleepers which are referred to above.'

A single image accompanied the article which was said to be on the Portsmouth (direct) main line.

Editor's comments: **We would be very interested to hear from readers who may have noted steel sleepers in use elsewhere. One line where we know they were in existence in the 1960s was on the single line of the Meon Valley route from Alton to at least its point of divergence at the erstwhile Butts Junction. How long they may have been present – cascaded perhaps from the Portsmouth line – is not known. Cascading and re-use of material was of course commonplace and we know sleepers and rails taken out of use on main lines might well find their way to secondary routes and further on sidings. Possibly electrification rendered steel sleepers unsuitable; there would certainly be issues when it came to track circuits. With grateful thanks to Peter Sikes who located the original article.**

From the archives: Shining a light on SR Publicity

Amyas Crump

Since the advent of public holidays, there have been those who invested in publicity to attract custom. Early adverts in the press might well be considered to be not quite up to the standards required today, but with photography available, images might well be provided that would give a much more accurate representation – or did they? (The old adage 'A picture speaks a thousand words' comes to mind.)

It is probably fair to suggest that the Great Western Railway were by the 1920s, the leaders amongst railway companies, in terms of their publicity output and yet, for all their many and varied books, booklets, puzzles, etc emanating from Paddington, one popular form of media seems to have escaped their attention and which in turn was instead picked up by the Southern. This was in the form of Magic Lantern based talks, presented at the time as both a widespread and popular form of both education and entertainment and typically used in the classroom, workplace and village hall from Edwardian times through to at least the mid-1960s – examples even exist of 1960s Magic Lantern slide publicity. For those more used to today's digital imagery, Magic Lanterns were an early form of projector (typically illuminated by oil or acetylene lamp although later the new-fangled electric lamp was provided). Slides were generally monochrome glass (some hand tinted), with colour appearing in line with changes in roll film. Size appears to have been standardised at 3¼" x 3⅛". Readers will no doubt be familiar with 35mm slides which were viewed from a projector with the image presented in a screen (or sheet or wall if you did not possess the latter). (Memories of wallpaper appearing as the backdrop to every slide or at the end catching one's fingers as the screen took on a life of its own.)

This untitled and undated image featuring a woman and child (they are present on the path) admiring the view, suggests a degree of artistic licence, particularly in regard to the colour of the sea! This bit of coast commences just east of Lyme Regis (Dorset) and extends past The Landslip (Dorset), Seaton, Sidmouth, Budleigh Salterton to Exmouth. With Dartmoor in the background. It is typical of the many charming holiday regions to which the Southern Railway provides access by express restaurant car trains.

THE UPLANDS OF DORSET

"There are dales in Dorset that are second to none in these islands, and heights full of the inscrutable mystery of the hills. The most haunting memory I have of this county is of a gorgeous landscape, seen in successive glimpses between Wareham and Wool, field and forest rising from a level plain and merging into the blue crests of Purbeck where they overhang the sea." D.M.

SOUTHERN RAILWAY
Wareham, Corfe Castle & Swanage stations are convenient for the Purbeck District and other parts of the "Hardy Country"
H. A. WALKER, General Manager.

Above: A rather more subdued and blandly colour washed scene. THE UPLANDS OF DORSET. There are dales in Dorset that are second to none in these islands, and heights full of the inscrutable mystery of the hills. The most haunting memory I have of this county is of a gorgeous landscape, seen in successive glimpses between Wareham and Wool, field and forest rising from a level plain and merging into the blue crests of Purbeck where they overhang the sea.

SOUTHERN RAILWAY Wareham, Corfe Castle & Swanage stations are convenient for the Purbeck District and other parts of the 'Hardy Country' : H. A. Walker, General Manager

Right: In a slightly different vein, a hand tinted, stylised advert for Charing Cross Hotel. Charing Cross Hotel is situated in the West End. Restaurant private rooms for luncheons and banquets. Phone Gerard 8025. A Southern Railway hotel. Telegrams – Banqueting Westrand London. There would also seem to have been a series promoting particular locations, but in absence of any definitive catalogue, there must surely be others? Readers' input will be welcomed. Noted examples are: DEAL Express Pullman service 2 hours from London. Through trains from North and Midlands (artwork by Pat Keely), The Londoner's garden – Kent (artwork by Gregory Brown), The Londoner's highlands – Surrey (artwork by Gregory Brown),The Londoner's leisure – the Thames.

One assumes that such images were once accompanied by notes, and it would be interesting to know if any survive, or even any advertising for such Magic Lantern shows, again, reader input would be welcome.

Waterloo in Colour: Steam, Diesel and Electric Images by Graham Smith courtesy Richard Sissons

Above: One of the final three Adams Radial tank engines, 4-4-2T No 30582, at Waterloo on 19 March 1961 in connection with the 'REC South Western Adams Radial Tank Tour'. This tour commenced and terminated at the terminus, a three coach train taking in several lines once regularly visited by the class when they had operated suburban trains prior to electrification.

Opposite top: West of England duty for No 35029 *Ellerman Lines* in September 1964. From the low number on the disc this was a Nine Elms duty. Alongside, the crew of a COR type set appear to be ready to join their own train.

Opposite bottom: Four months earlier, Graham had recorded the engine from an earlier arrival trailing its coaches – rather closely perhaps – to the end of the platform at which point it will wait until the signal clears, allowing a return to Nine Elms for servicing. Underneath the grime there is a green engine, somewhere, possibly identified as No 34034 *Honiton.*

35029
15
35029

Top: Simultaneous steam departures; in the background a Class 4 tank on empty stock from a recent arrival bound for Clapham Junction, whilst nearest the camera Nos 31791 and 31639 have charge of an RCTS special destined for Longmoor which the pair will take as far as Woking. And eventually reconnect with at Windsor & Eton Riverside on the return journey, 30 April 1966.

Bottom: Setting off for Southampton, No 34021 *Dartmoor* will be making that characteristic soft chuffing sound so typical of the Bulleid breed. The man painting the 'MIND THE GAP' signs is oblivious to what is happening behind him whilst further back an electric set, HAP perhaps, may well be on an Esher race-day special. (We are well aware this image was used in ST1 but the request had come to see it again in larger format.)

Opposite top: Two Bulleid engines both possibly awaiting return to Nine Elms; Nos 35005 *Canadian Pacific* and an unidentified machine. Between both is one of the short bays where the station pilots would stand awaiting their next move; the man at track level possibly shovelling ashes. In the far background at what were then storage sidings are electric units awaiting their next duty.

Opposite bottom: Quite possibly taken a few minutes after the view of 35029 seen earlier. The train now getting away whilst again in the background an ECS move, this time behind a Class 2, is getting away.

35005

WB.157
WB 158
35029
GUARD

80137
3123
80

62

Opposite top: A typically busy day at Waterloo with alternate steam and electric, recorded in June 1965. No 80137 is ready for an ECS working when next required; possibly having already 'shoved' a departing train and come to rest at the end of the now deserted platform. Alongside, 4-COR No 3123 heads a Portsmouth semi-fast, and finally No 34077 *603 Squadron* also awaits departure. (The second COR type set beyond this is not identified.)

Opposite bottom: Salisbury semi-fast awaiting departure from Waterloo post-steam: '33 and TC set'. Somehow a far cry from when a steam hauled train of perhaps 8-10 coaches might have been used. But times were changing and likewise appearances , notice the new office 'raft' built across the end of the platforms. This in turn would free up the main buildings allowing the latter to be rented out for office and retail use.

This page, top: Waterloo in April 1970. A Class 33, the General Manager's saloon, and further across a blue painted COR – surely green was better for these sets. The saloon, unless it has just arrived at the rear of a train and which from the absence of a tail lamp appears unlikely, will be propelled either by a Class 33 or Class 73. The number '94' not explained.

This page, bottom: We hesitate to say Waterloo in modern times as even this image was taken getting on for two decades ago. Visit the same location today and assuming you are not arrested for taking a photograph, the stock has again all changed. The greatest loss is probably the excellent Wessex Electric sets, popular with passengers and which so nearly had a renaissance a few years ago – sadly now all scrapped. Sir Herbert Walker would never have had grass in the 'six-foot' at his terminus even it was in green in colour!

One of the three named steam engines referred to by Frank Box in his article. This is No 30452 Sir Meliagrance, this time in BR days at Nine Elms on 6 September 1958. No 30452, and sister No 30771 Sir Sagramore behind, are arriving at the depot having reversed from Waterloo and then been routed in the depot from Loco Junction signal box in the background. Appropriately No 30453 displays a West of England headcode. *R. C. Riley / The Transport Treasury*

Into BR days, No 34081 *92 Squadron* entering Yeoford on 26 May 1961 with the 8.10 am Salisbury to Ilfracombe service, 26 May 1961. *Leslie Freeman / Transport Treasury*

The 10.35am Waterloo to Ilfracombe

The Southern lines west of Exeter have ever been a magnet for interest. Notwithstanding the recent welcome reinstatement of regular services to Okehampton, much of what once was remains devoid of rails although we still hope that one day common sense will prevail and Okehampton to Bere Alston may yet become a reality together with Bodmin to Wadebridge.

Attempting to pick a favourite amongst the standard gauge lines is both difficult and dangerous; Padstow perhaps because of its proximity to the coast, Halwill for its diversity in workings, or Ilfracombe, high above the town and the need for superlative effort by an engine on the steep gradients either side of the approach summit.

As to the reason why these and other lines in the area were closed we have to look back to the 1960s and 1970s – I have deliberately not mentioned the dreaded 'B' word as we must also be honest and say the Southern had long regarded the lines west of Exeter as a drain on resources and there is the oft quoted saying from folklore that Waterloo would be delighted if they could persuade Paddington to take them on!

That wish would indeed come true two generations ago but at a time when economy was the order of the day and the various regional managers were faced with stark choices. 'You have "x" pounds in the budget. How you use it is up to you.' What that meant in reality was subsidise loss making lines or modernise elsewhere. Small wonder they chose the latter and which was far more likely to generate a better return on investment. Consequently the various former Southern lines were literally left to wither and die, a desultory passenger service now shunned by travellers who found the alterative bus or private car more convenient and consequently more attractive.

Writing this in 2022 we might well hope for some of the reinstatements described above, although that from Barnstaple to Ilfracombe would appear one of the least likely to ever see trains again.

Co-incidentally, thumbing through the 1937 *Southern Railway Magazine,* we came across an article by the late Frank E. Box on the accelerated service from Waterloo to the North Devon town. We had also made a promise to several who had recently kindly written in to comment on the puzzle picture from Issue 2 (Scotland? – no, Barnstaple), to include something on the 'Withered Arm', hence we hope you enjoy it.

'The 10.35am Waterloo to Ilfracombe'

It was 62 years ago in July 1874 that the railway was opened to Ilfracombe, when the fastest train, the 2.10 pm from Waterloo, occupied 7 hours 18 minutes on the journey. During the following 31 years the service was gradually improved and in the summer of 1905 the 10.40 am reached Ilfracombe in 5 hours 12 minutes. The booking of this train was interesting, as no stops were scheduled at either of the Exeter stations, a timing of 71 minutes being instituted for the 52 miles from Sidmouth Junction to Barnstaple Junction. During a second period of 31 years until last summer, however, no material improvement took place in the fastest Down service. Except for the lean years during and following the war, a journey time of about 5½ hours became more or less stabilised for the principal Down train. It will be conceded therefore that the acceleration promised for 1936 was at least due, and it was with keen anticipation that the writer awaited the issue of the timetables, which revealed an acceleration of the 10.35 am by 13 minutes on the booking of 1935 - and on that of the 10.40 am in 1905*.

In the reverse direction a timing. of 5 hr. 10 min. by the 10.30 am from Ilfracombe first came into operation in the summer of 1935 and was continued in 1936. The issue of the public timetable book has lately been commendably early and the re-drafting of the West of England tables, by the incorporation of the whole of the Western main line services in

Ascending the fearsome 1 in 36 of Mortehoe bank in the Up direction on 16 May 1958. A pair of Southern moguls, one at least recorded as No 31849, are coupled smokebox to smokebox for the climb. With turning facilities available at Ilfracombe it is slightly strange that both engines were not facing the same way. *A. E. Bennett / Transport Treasury*

one table, and by the elimination of the connecting road services, has resulted in a great gain in clarity and in ease of reference. One small error, persistent for some ten years, still remains; the Barnstaple Junction mileage is shown as 210½ - instead of 211½.

On the morning of 6 July, the writer set forth hopefully to observe and record the first journey of the accelerated 10.35 am, which was scheduled to reach Exeter in 3 hr. 7 min. and Ilfracombe in 4 hr. 57 min., and with an 86 min. booking to Salisbury, 83¾ miles, to provide the Southern Railway with its fastest start to stop run at 58.5 mph. Doubts - unfortunately justified - as to the prospect of time-keeping to Salisbury arose, for not only was the West of England train closely preceded, as in former years, by the 10.30 am 'Bournemouth Belle', but at 10.33 am a Guildford electric was also interposed between the two expresses. No. 856, *Lord St. Vincent*, was at the head of the train, which was made up of four coaches for Ilfracombe, two for Torrington, four (including restaurant car) for Padstow, and two for Bude, in all taring 387 tons, or 32 tons in excess of the loading for which the "timing was arranged".

The right-away signal was received punctually, perhaps somewhat unfortunately as *Lord Anson*, with the 'Bournemouth Belle', had left barely two minutes ahead. There is little of interest to record as far as Salisbury. A moderate start was made, adverse signals were met with at Malden and again approaching milepost 30, while throughout to Worting the running was no doubt restrained in view of the train ahead. Beyond the point of divergence no attempt was apparently made to retrieve any of the six minutes which had been lost, and the train rolled into Salisbury this amount late in 92 min. 2 sec. at 12.7¼ pm. The minimum speeds beyond Worting and

Grateley were 48.9 and 30 mph. respectively, and maximums of 81.8 Down into Andover and 77.6 beyond Porton were recorded.

At Salisbury hopes again became in the ascendant as an old friend, No. 452, *Sir Meliagrance,* backed on to the 387 tons train. Leaving 6 min. 39 sec. late in a nasty drizzle more or less intermittent as far as Axminster - the opening to Dinton was fair, Semley was breasted in good style, but in spite of 78 mph. before Templecombe, a minimum of 46.4 mph. at mp. 113½-, and 80 mph. just attained down Sherborne bank, the gain on schedule at Yeovil Junction was a mere five seconds. Sutton Bingham bank was topped at 52.3 mph. and with 70.3 mph. before Crewkerne, and a minimum of 37.5 mph. before Hewish, excellent progress was now made, Chard Junction being passed in 59 min. 25 sec. at 79 mph.

At the foot of the long downhill stretch speed had risen to 84.1 mph. at mp. 146½, and it was still 62.5 mph. on the 1 in 80 up beyond Seaton Junction at mp. 148½, to fall to 31.9 at mp. 151, and to a minimum of 23.9 at 152¼ before entering the tunnel. Beyond, 84.1 mph. was again touched at mp. 158½ and with 83.3 mph. after Whimple an arrival at Exeter in 92 minutes was anticipated, but brakes were applied before Broad Clyst and speed was rapidly reduced for a pw check at Pinhoe, whereby about 2.1 minutes were lost. The clock at Exeter Central showed 1.47 pm, five minutes late, as *Sir Meliagrance* came to a standstill in 94 min. 20 sec. (92 min. net.) from Salisbury.

The overall time from London was 3 hr. 11 min. 41 sec., so the new schedule of 3 hr. 7 min. had been exceeded by 4¾ minutes, but delays had accounted for over 8 min. The net running time was about 178 minutes. At Exeter the division of the train was effected smartly, and leaving the Padstow and Bude portions behind, the six North Devon coaches (192 tons) drawn by No. 1830, a 2-6-0, departed

Left: Southern termini: 226 miles 39 chains from Waterloo. (Only Bude at 228 miles 20 chains, and Padstow at 259 miles 50 chains were further away.) The station here was one of those Dr Beeching did not approve of. A limited regular clientele bolstered during the summer season. To cater for the latter, engines and coaches would perhaps stand idle for up to eight months of the year, we cannot deny this was hardly an economic use of resources. As if to prove the point we only have to look at the history of the all-Pullman 'Devon Belle' service introduced by the Southern Railway in June 1947. Originally consisting of two portions split at Exeter, one for Plymouth and the second for Ilfracombe, the service did not attract the patronage anticipated and the Plymouth portion was dropped as early as September 1949. Further cuts so as to make the Ilfracombe train a summer only service took place in 1952 but even this was insufficient and the train ceased to run after the summer timetable of 1954. *Transport Treasury*

Right: Seen from the cab of a Western Region DMU approaching the station, almost the full extent of the resources available are laid bare – the engine shed and turntable are out of camera to the right. The numerous carriage sidings on the right would at times be full but in this undated view it seems such occasions may be in the past. *Transport Treasury*

just over 4 min. late. Making a stay of 2½ min. at St. Davids, time was thence steadily gained, and, the Portsmouth Arms 'conditional' not being made, Barnstaple Junction was reached only 1¾ min. late.

After the two Torrington vehicles had been detached, No. 1830 with the remaining four coaches, 128 tons, reached Braunton 1 min. 24 sec. late, but here the station allowance was exceeded by 1 min., and, a very gentle ascent of the steep Braunton Bank being made, hopes of recording a punctual arrival at Ilfracombe were dwindling. Mortehoe, however, did well and despatched us in nearly a minute under its allotted time. Soon afterwards the short tunnel at Slade was threaded, and at 3.30 pm the station at Ilfracombe, half-a-mile away, came in sight. The final drop, which still continues at 1 in 36 for some distance along the length of the platform, was negotiated with the usual caution, and it was 3 hr, 31 min, 45 sec. pm.as mp. 226 near the end of the platform was passed.

So, very nearly on time, the train was slowly brought to a standstill at 3 hr. 32 min. 38 sec. pm, 38 sec. late, but only 20 sec. over the new 4 hr. 57 min. schedule from Waterloo. This will be considered as near enough to absolute punctuality as not to matter, yet a shade more energy on the Braunton bank would have ensured an arrival exactly on time on this journey, which in a sense was historic, as initiating a booking within five hours.

A second trip was made some weeks later which afforded distinct contrasts to the journey just described. On this occasion time was kept on each section, but perhaps the best locomotive work was done on the Waterloo-Salisbury run by No. 781, *Sir Aglovale*, with 11 coaches 355 tons tare. Leaving 1½ min. late - 5 min. after the 'Belle' - the running was again restrained as far as Worting Junction. Slight signal slacks were experienced at Raynes Park and beyond Farnborough, but the total loss was only about ¾ min. The opening was somewhat better than that of No. 856, and 68.2 mph. was reached after Weybridge, followed by a minimum of 48.9 at mp. 31. Worting Junction was passed in 55 min. 22 sec.= 1 min. 22 sec. over schedule - the minimum just beyond being 54.2 mph. The work now appreciated considerably and the 16.1 miles from Worting to Andover Junction were run in the fast time of 13 min. 56 sec. with a maximum of 84.9 mph. before Andover. Thence to Tunnel Junction, 161 miles, took only 14 min. 19 sec. with the high minimum of 55.5 mph beyond Grateley and a maximum down Porton of 81.8 mph. The train drew up at Salisbury in 86 min. 3 sec. or in about 85¾ min. net, so the arrears at Worting had been recovered.

Here No. 452 *Sir Meliagrance* again took charge, and still 1½ min. late, made an uneventful, albeit well judged run. Although nearly ½ min was gained on the 96 min. schedule to Exeter, the uphill minima were slightly lower than on the first trip, while 80 mph. was not attained at any point apart from a momentary, and somewhat doubtful, 80.4 mph. recorded for one quarter-mile beyond Whimple. The arrival at Exeter was at 1 hr. 43 min. 7 sec. pm, just over 1 min. late, the actual time from Salisbury being 95 min. 36 sec.

The departures from both stations at Exeter were still the initial 1½ min. late, but No. 1496 with 5 coaches, 160 tons, taking things easily, would have recorded a punctual arrival at Barnstaple Junction, if signals at Chapelton had not intervened, so it was 2 hr. 48 min. 16 sec. pm (1¾ min. late) when the train drew up at the Junction station. Again, the departure would have been on time, but for some rather dilatory passengers transferring from the Up Bideford line train; as it was, this slight delay caused the maximum lateness at any one point on this trip, viz., 1 min, 50 sec, However, with but 3 coaches, 96 tons, a more forceful climb in 13 min. 35 sec., station to station, of the Braunton bank made the train two minutes early at Mortehoe, and getting away from this somewhat bleak spot a few seconds in advance of 'advertised time', No. 1496 cautiously drew up at Ilfracombe at 3 hr 28 min. 50 sec. pm, or in 4 hr, 52 min, 13 sec, from Waterloo.

Thus a late departure of 1 min, 37 sec, had been turned into an early arrival of 3 min. 10 secs. mainly by virtue of the spirited climb up to Mortehoe. To the locomotive staff on these journeys - who were not aware that they were being timed - the writer would express his thanks for these interesting runs. On this last trip, as also on a later one by the 10.35 am, to Salisbury only, made early in September, the trains were in charge of Guard S. G. Coulson, to whom on his retirement at the end of September, after 50 years of service with the LSWR and SR, the writer would wish many long and happy years.

The September journey to Salisbury with No. 851 *Sir Francis Drake*, 11 coaches, 356 tons tare, was disappointing as 4 min. 20 sec. were dropped in spite of an 'electrifying' start to Clapham Junction and an unchecked run. The first milepost was passed in 2 min, 27 sec., Vauxhall in 3 min, 1 sec, and 52.3 mph was attained at mp. 2¾. Clapham was passed in 6 min. 13 sec, but after easing through the station recovery was poor, and Surbiton took 14 min, 59 sec. Woking 27 min, 55 sec, and Worting Junction 56 min, 27 sec. Although space - not to mention exhaustion of the readers' patience - prevents a description of the return journeys, the writer would like this account to have a happy ending, so he will conclude by stating that the best performances in the Up direction were between Salisbury and Waterloo; No. 862 *Lord Collingwood*, with 355 tons taking 84 min. 49 sec. and No. 2331 *Beattie* - name of happy memories -with 314 tons, 85 min, 51 sec (85¼ net). Time, however, was gained by all the engines and punctuality in most cases was strictly maintained.

* The 10.35 a.m. from Waterloo runs in the summer service, and from Mondays to Fridays carries the North Devon and North Cornwall portions of the 'Atlantic Coast Express'. On Saturdays the train is further subdivided, the 10.35 am running to Ilfracombe, the 10.45 am to Padstow and the 11.0 am to Plymouth, Bude and Torrington. In the winter service the 'Atlantic Coast Express' leaves at 11.0 am for all parts.

Beyond the end of the sidings is a sheer drop, the town and the beach fronting the Bristol Channel. A resurgence at Ilfracombe is sadly unlikely but we can at least dream. *Transport Treasury.*

Guildford (and its environs) Part 1

Colin Martin

Colin Martin has been a friend of 'Southern Times' and 'other' journals for many years. His collection reposes with the Transport Treasury so we also thought it appropriate we presented a selection of his images both at Guildford and nearby.

Times change, and whilst almost everything depicted has long disappeared we should still be grateful for two things; firstly the actual railway survives, and secondly Colin was around to record matters before the 'modern' railway arrived upon the scene.

Top: We start with electric an at Godalming. 2-BIL set No 2017 working a stopping service on the Portsmouth line.

Middle: This time we are at Wanborough on the Guildford to Reading line and where N No 31858 is displaying the usual two disc route code but with the addition of an oil lamp in between. Forgotten by the crew perhaps?

Bottom: At the south end of the station we have a panoramic view of the tunnel, the engine shed and the south signal box. The EMU arriving at the station is on another Portsmouth line stopping service.

Opposite Top: Now to steam which will be the dominant feature of this piece. U No 31798 on the approaches to Guildford with a local working – it also proves the point not all passenger services were electric!

Opposite Bottom: On to Woplesdon, with Standard 4 2-6-4T No 80137 at Worplesdon. (Recall John Davenport's recollections about the Down distant signal here in WW2 in this issue – see page 44.)

We regret we have simply run of space in this issue. Part 2 of a selection of Colin's images in Southern Times No 5.

Treasures from the Bluebell Railway Museum
Tony Hillman

When the London and South Western Railway introduced its electric train services, the traditional train route indication of discs attached to the front of a steam locomotive was replaced on the front of an EMU by a letter to show the route. This practice was continued by the Southern Railway (SR) past 1923.

A few years later a connection was made with an article in the January 1922 'South Western Railway Magazine' describing some new advertisements being installed in coaches.

'Railway Carriage Advertising'

'During the past month many of the staff travelling on the suburban electrified services will have observed that certain of the photochrom *views displayed in compartments have been replaced by artistically designed and produced commercial advertisements.*

'These changes are the result of the decision of the Directors to offer the very valuable advertising spaces in the electrical stock to firms of repute, and that a high artistic standard has been created is evident by the tasteful designs of the advertisements which have already been fitted.'

Unfortunately, the article does not go on to list the companies, but it is very likely that Hovis was one. This early advertisement predates the SR one below so was either in late LSWR or early SR electrics.

A later article in the successor to the 'South Western Railway Magazine', the October 1926 'Southern Railway Magazine', describes a new advertisement.

'Topical Advertising'

'The Hovis Bread Company has recently issued a clever and attractive advertisement, which is exhibited in Southern electric coaches. The word "Hovis" is formed by the headcodes carried by certain electric trains, viz:

H = Hampton Court

Ō = Hounslow

V = Kingston (Thames Valley)

I = Dorking North

S = Shepperton

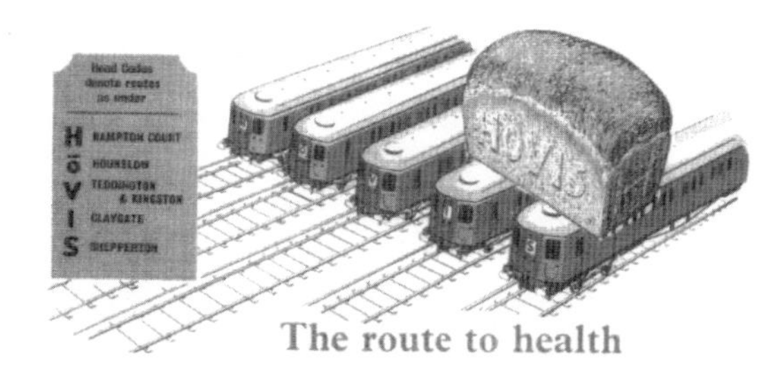

Early version of the 'HOVIS' advertisement with LSWR destination letters respectfully for Hampton Court, Hounslow, Teddington & Kingston, Claygate, Shepperton and 'The route to health' slogan.

It is interesting to note that all the routes shown are ex-LSWR lines as by October 1926, and with the electrified network expanding, other SR routes could have been used.

The tild or bar (sometimes also referred to as a macron) above the letter O was used by Hovis advertisements in 1920 and later. Letter O with bar shows the route Waterloo - Waterloo via Richmond and Hounslow. Without the bar the route is reversed.

The magazine advertisement shown is from 1936.

A version of the same advertisement but appearing as a carriage print was produced later although this time the tild O has been removed. Note also, the 'Go b(u)y it' phrase has appeared. This time non ex-LSWR routes

have also been included. The routes shown are:

H Victoria – Hayes, Hampton Court

O Orpington, Hounslow

V Epsom, Dartford, Kingston

I Coulsdon North, Beckenham Junction Dorking

S Sutton, Dartford, Shepperton

Finally, in 1947 Hovis and the Southern Railway produced five carriage prints showing

baker's shops in towns in Kent and Sussex. The artwork was by David Burley. As well as the Rye print shown, similar prints were made for Cuckfield and Rotherfield in Sussex along with Cranbrook and Westerham in Kent.
This print is on display in the Museum and others, along with the HOVIS carriage print, are on view in the carriages of the Bluebell Railway.

Five original headcode plates from Southern electric trains are on display in the Bluebell Railway Museum.

My thanks go to Colin Chivers and Eric Penn who provided the 'Route to Health and 'Go b(u)y it' images

Next time from the Bluebell Museum Archive:
A 'coming together' of a Bulleid and a Well-tank at Wadebridge

Continuing with the Bluebell Museum Archive, and similarly from 'Any Questions' to 'Any Answers' (with due acknowledgment to the BBC.

Thanks to the Correspondents who responded to the Mystery Photo in Southern Times 3. The train is on double track which means it either between Okehampton and Meldon Junction or on the short section of double track south of Halwill Junction by the WW2 Military Sidings. While the topology of each area is very similar the rails on the 'other' track are very shiny, not as would be expected in the sidings loop. The train can therefore be confirmed as having left Okehampton on its way to Meldon. The sloping bridge in the background, between the chimney and dome, is the one now known as Tors Road Bridge. If you stood on this bridge and looked towards Okehampton you would see where the Surbiton to Okehampton Car Carrier service was stabled.

Martin James has also written having also studied the image. He states:

1. 30283 was based at Exmouth Junction until November 1950 so that fits in with the photo's date of 24th of June 1950 - which was a Saturday. (A pity the sun was not out - a shadow would have been useful to confirm the time of day.)

2. The headcode is for Exeter Central to Padstow

3. Normally the stock would be two 2P-sets but the train has a 2P-set for Padstow and a Bulleid brake composite (loose) to Diagram 2406 and a Maunsell corridor third for Bude. (. Vans were added to any train west of Exeter Central.)

4. The train is on double track which puts it between Okehampton and Meldon Junction - beyond Meldon Junction the line was single track to Padstow with passing loops only at stations.

5. The train appears to be taking a long left bend and is still climbing. The houses in the distance are probably on the outskirts of Okehampton.

6. Looking at the OS map, I believe that the train is south-and-slightly-west of Okehampton Castle / south of Okehampton Golf Club and the photo is taken from where the modern A30 Okehampton bypass is - just before the line now goes under the modern A30 in a long bridge.

T9 No 30283.

Bluebell Museum Image Ref: 040942

From the footplate

We start this collection with a note from **John Wenyon** re **ST2**. 'On page 11 it shows a forlorn looking Pacific, No 34035, at Eastleigh works yard. My supposition is that this loco was withdrawn with mechanical problems but still had a good boiler and so was positioned where it is shown to provide steam to the works safety valve test house; the take-off isolating valve can be seen just above the loco next to the test house silencer/muffler steel chimney on the roof of the test house, a corner of which can just be seen. This was a single storey brick building. not very imposing but with the silencer very visible on the roof.

'The Bullied Pacifics were favourites for this duty, partly because they had large boilers capable of putting a safety valve through a vigorous accumulation test to see what pressure would rise to once they had started to lift, and they had been stressed to operate at 280 p.s.i. when first built so there was a safe margin over the then normal maximum operating pressure of 250 p.s.i.

'I only spent a day working with the test house staff, but the procedure seemed to be to set up an overhauled safety valve on the test rig, close the door from the operators' room. (I think there was a glass viewing panel to see the action without being deafened!) The loco fireman would then be instructed as to the pressure to aim for, the test house steam valve would be opened and we would wait until the safety valve lifted. If the pressure as seen on the calibrated test house pressure gauge needed adjusting, the safety valve would be isolated and the loco fireman asked to reduce steam pressure a bit (put on injectors perhaps?). The test would be repeated with the loco boiler pressure being constantly adjusted until the test house staff were satisfied, whereupon the safety valve adjustments would be sealed and its operating pressure stamped upon it. It would then be available for an overhauled loco as required in the erecting or boiler shop.

'Somewhere there must be documents defining the operating procedures for the test house and perhaps even drawings showing the whole installation.

'On the day I was there, the loco providing steam had a two man crew. A boring duty perhaps but still easier than firing up to Waterloo.'

John Wenyon, C.M.&E.E. student in 1964.

Next from **Colin Turtle,** again re **Issue 2**. 'With reference to the interesting set of pictures in Issue 2, "Interlude around Midhurst," at least one of that station's target signs was reused at Mitcham Junction on the Up platform, under the canopy.

'I discovered this by chance. In the reflected light, the silhouette of the original "Midhurst" name could be seen under the "Mitcham Junction" name. There may have been other target signs from the same origin, but I didn't check further at the time. I made this observation on one of the many times I changed at Mitcham Junction during the journey to and from school at Sutton, from Merton Park during 1959-61. The Southern Railway was noted for its wise reuse of everything and this shows how this fine tradition was continued by the Southern Region.'

Next from **Trevor Hodgson,** partly on the same topic of Smoke Defectors, etc **(ST2)** but with a little more as well.

'I noticed in the first article on smoke deflectors, a group picture on page 12 showing the people involved and I note that neither of the footplate crew are named. However, I can at least identify the driver to the left of Harry Frith and with his SR Engineman's cap badge. This is Reg Woods who was responsible for getting me started on my railway career back in 1973.

'I worked with Reg at Eastleigh and he would often bring in photos to show me of engines he had taken out on test after having been rebuilt or as in this case, on test. Most of these trial runs were on the Eastleigh to Fareham line where they might, if necessary, stop in section perhaps to check on something but without disrupting the ordinary traffic too much. It was under these conditions that Reg would take his pictures. It would appear from what I remember he was the chosen man for this work, he must have been one of the senior drivers at Eastleigh, as I recall he told me he had started on the LSWR about 1914.'

We asked Trevor what else he might recall of Reg and he responded, 'Yes dear old Reg Woods, you would liked to have met him, lovely man, always happy and smiling. When I turned to that page and saw him posing against the engine I immediately recognised him, and many thoughts went through my mind.

'As you say what a pity I did not ask him more questions and record better what he said, instead of just memories which like all of us fade over time.

'The last time I met him was over 45 years ago now but his image is still clear in my mind and the day he brought me the cutting out of the newspaper to apply for a job on the railway still resonates with me, so turning that page in issue two just brought loads of memories back to me, he looked just the same as when I knew him ten years later. 'I recall him bringing photos in to show me of engines on test and some I clearly remember as being in works grey livery, all rebuilt Pacifics.

'I often wondered over the years what might have happened to his photos and negatives but he had a son he used to visit every few months who lived up in Shoeburyness so hopefully he might have given them a home, I would certainly like to see them myself.

'A couple of things I do clearly recall. His favourite engine was No 755 *The Red Knight*. With the large diameter chimney this was a strong engine. He also told me the story, which I cannot now remember, as to how the 700 class got their nickname of Black Motors.

'On a more sombre note he also told me about the death of his father who I believe was a driver as well. One cold winter's day he was walking across the front of the shed at Eastleigh and a northerly wind was blowing accompanied by snow. Sadly he was hit by an engine backing into the shed. They did what they could and loaded him into a van, probably an LSWR road van, to take him to hospital in Southampton where he later died of his injuries.'

Several readers have also kindly written in to comment upon the not-deliberately intended **'mystery picture'** in **Issue 2**. No it is not Scotland but is in fact Barnstaple Junction.

John Bradbeer is typical with his comments, 'Just got the latest issue of (ST2) and only opened as far as page 2 so far! The location of the photo with No 32096 is Barnstaple Junction, at the southern (Up) end of platform 1.

SOUTHERN REGION STATIONS

Can you guess the names? As a clue to start you off, they are stations in (1) Isle of Wight; (2) Kent; (3) Hampshire; and (4) Sussex. See page 192 for answers.

Just for amusement, can you identify the four stations depicted in these cartoons from 1949? In order the counties involved are the Isle of Wight, Kent, Hampshire, and Sussex. Answers next time.

The loco is standing at the coaling siding on the track to the right is a siding leading to the goods shed (behind the photographer). Although there is a platform edge, this was never given a platform number and no passenger trains left from it, although there was a Mortehoe to Waterloo summer Saturday train that collected a restaurant car from the platform. I must have spent many hours at or near this spot in the early 1960s.

'The headcode is from Duty 579, which had the loco on station pilot and yard duty at Barnstaple Junction, with a trip to Fremington to shunt wagons on the quay for the afternoon. I see that 32096 went from Barnstaple Junction to Plymouth Friary in June 1955 before being withdrawn from Friary in November 1956. So your picture has to be before 1955 (and that was about when I first got taken to Barnstaple Junction to watch the trains!).'

Others who came up with the same and to whom we extend our thanks are Martin James, Roger Merry-Price, and Tony Hillman.

The Editor(s) are pleased to receive comments, plaudits and brickbats but reserve the right to edit comments as necessary. Views of contributors do not necessarily represent the views of the Editors or Publisher.